"Dr Devis-Rozental offers practic
The Student Wellbeing Toolkit is
evidence-based research with cl
prove useful to students and prof
their needs and boundaries, and hc

Claudia Röhlen,
MSc Positive Psychology and Programme manager
at the Drive Forward Foundation

"As a dyslexic educator, I've struggled with academic texts. *The Student Wellbeing Toolkit* is relatable and easily digestible. If you're feeling overwhelmed, lost or clueless about starting university, I'd recommend you read this book. It's a MUST read for students and educators in higher education."

Nathaniel Hawley,
Head of Community, Exceptional Individuals

"Dr Devis-Rozental has prepared a brilliant quest to help you reach self-actualisation, she will armour you with the knowledge of wellbeing – whether that may be socially, physically, financially or emotionally. Make sure you get your hands on this book!"

Fiifi Asafu-Adjaye,
SUBU Vice President Student Opportunities

The Student Wellbeing Toolkit

The Student Wellbeing Toolkit puts wellbeing at the centre of your journey into university and beyond. By encouraging self-efficacy and a focus on the things you can control, it provides clear guidance to enhance wellbeing and opportunities for self-reflection that help develop self-awareness and prosocial skills for life.

Offering an accessible toolkit of strategies, activities and tips this fantastic, accessible resource considers wellbeing within six main areas:

- Physical wellbeing
- Socio-emotional wellbeing
- Intellectual wellbeing
- Environmental wellbeing
- Occupational wellbeing
- Financial wellbeing

Drawing on research-evidenced theories around positive psychology, theories of learning, motivation and self-development, the book explores what, how and why these areas are key to our wellbeing and the rationale for taking them into account to enable you to flourish and thrive at university.

Camila Devis-Rozental (DProf) is an award-winning educator and author with expertise in socio-emotional intelligence as well as student wellbeing and success. Dr Devis-Rozental is principal academic at Bournemouth University, UK.

Routledge Study Skills

The Student Wellbeing Toolkit
Preparing for Life at College, University and Beyond
Camila Devis-Rozental

Writing a Postgraduate Thesis or Dissertation
Tools for Success
Michael Hammond

Studying Online
Succeeding through Distance Learning at University
Graham Jones

For more information about this series, please visit: www.routledge.com/Routledge-Study-Skills/book-series/ROUTLEDGESS

The Student Wellbeing Toolkit

Preparing for Life at College, University and Beyond

Camila Devis-Rozental

Routledge
Taylor & Francis Group

LONDON AND NEW YORK

Designed cover image: © Shutterstock

First published 2023
by Routledge
4 Park Square, Milton Park, Abingdon, Oxon OX14 4RN

and by Routledge
605 Third Avenue, New York, NY 10158

Routledge is an imprint of the Taylor & Francis Group, an informa business

© 2023 Camila Devis-Rozental

The right of Camila Devis-Rozental to be identified as author of this work
has been asserted in accordance with sections 77 and 78 of the Copyright,
Designs and Patents Act 1988.

British Library Cataloguing-in-Publication Data
A catalogue record for this book is available from the British Library

Library of Congress Cataloging-in-Publication Data
Names: Devis-Rozental, Camila, author.
Title: The student wellbeing toolkit : preparing for life at college, university
    and beyond / Camila Devis-Rozental.
Description: Abingdon, Oxon ; New York, NY : Routledge, 2023. | Series:
    Routledge study skills | Includes bibliographical references and index.
Identifiers: LCCN 2022057482 (print) | LCCN 2022057483 (ebook) |
    ISBN 9781032329659 (hardback) | ISBN 9781032329666 (paperback) |
    ISBN 9781003317548 (ebook)
Subjects: LCSH: College students—Life skills guides. | College students—
    Conduct of life. | College students—Health and hygiene. | Well-being.
Classification: LCC LB3609 .D48 2023 (print) | LCC LB3609 (ebook) |
    DDC 378.1/98—dc23/eng/20230215
LC record available at https://lccn.loc.gov/2022057482
LC ebook record available at https://lccn.loc.gov/2022057483

ISBN: 978-1-032-32965-9 (hbk)
ISBN: 978-1-032-32966-6 (pbk)
ISBN: 978-1-003-31754-8 (ebk)

DOI: 10.4324/9781003317548

Typeset in Warnock Pro
by Apex CoVantage, LLC

To my children, Dani and David; my nephews, Francisco, Joaquin, Osher, Raphael, Leo and Milo; and my godson, Sebastian, remember that you are the writer of your story. I hope this book inspires you to make it a good one!

Contents

Figures

Tables

Foreword

'85

When I look back, I think 1985 was my favourite year. I was 16, and I felt that the world was opening up to me and my friends. It was a time when life seemed full of possibilities but also fears, the strange juxtaposition of opportunity and the unknown. We all have a "best year" growing up, one we all look back on with a smile, maybe a smirk and a sense of if only . . . Ask your parents what year it was for them . . . Here's a thought, what if you are living in yours now?

In '85:

Ronald Reagan was President of the US, and Margaret Thatcher was the British Prime Minister.

Music by Prince, Madonna, Duran Duran and Sade was what we were listening to.

Back to the Future, Rambo 2, Rocky 4 and *Beverly Hills Cop* were the films we were talking about and sneaking into underage.

The original Live Aid lit up the summer; the biggest global concert ever, and I was there!

The environment was in the news after French agents sank Greenpeace's ship, the *Rainbow Warrior*, in New Zealand.

Nintendo launched their games system NES, and with it, *Super Mario* was born.

Michael Jordan slammed onto the sports scene, being named rookie of the year in the NBA.

Ruth Lawrence made all teenagers look bad by becoming the youngest person ever to get a First Class Honours Degree in Mathematics from the University of Oxford, aged 13!

We were living with a global pandemic, AIDS.

Microsoft launched their first Windows, and the average annual salary was around £9000 or $16000US.

It was the year I started my life's to-do list. I remember the first time I thought about it, I was sat on my bedroom windowsill at about 11pm on a summer's evening in my home, in North West London, looking out at the shimmering lights, the cars and buildings. I had a great view; we were on top of a hill, and on that evening, in that moment, it looked like I could see the whole of London, in fact, the whole world.

I was in a thoughtful mood, one of those moments where you lose yourself in contemplation and fantasy.

Out there, I thought, was potentially the person I would fall in love with and maybe grow old with, was my first job, my first home . . . my future!

Until I was 14, I had wanted to be a lawyer. I loved the idea of standing in a courtroom and defending an innocent person, but the romance of it was shattered when in that summer, I got to spend a few weeks shadowing my mum's divorce lawyer, Mrs Langham. Two things struck me by the end of the experience; firstly, that the job wasn't that sexy. It was mainly bloody hard work, lots of reading and meetings; and secondly, I didn't think I was anywhere near clever enough. Daily, I heard Mrs Langham and her colleagues speaking a language I barely understood.

By the time I was sat on that windowsill in '85, I wanted to be an actor, or a writer, or both. It was something I was good at and was the thing that I believed defined me; it was my thing! I wasn't good at sports, so I wasn't in with those kids; I wasn't academically the smartest, so those kids intimidated me; I was average; too skinny, too self-conscious and not particularly funny or charismatic, but give me a script and a character to inhabit, and I was away!

My "to-do list" included getting through the next two years at school and then getting out of education to work in the arts. I was at quite a posh school, so my friends and peers were all about university. In hindsight, I think I chose not to be, not because I didn't want to go but because I was so scared of trying and failing that as a result, I persuaded myself to try a different path, one I felt I could achieve on and therefore avoid the ignominy of missing out . . .

'85 was the year, though; all that shimmered that night was gold, and everything ahead was possible. Although, there were moments of anxiety, of fear; of leaving the warm familiarity of my school, my friends, my routines, but that was still two years away, somewhere that was still on the abstract horizon.

In '85, I truly believed that my life would map out smoothly and that I would be acting on Broadway or in the West End by the time I was 20 and that I would have won an Oscar by 30.

As the sun came up the next morning and I began the "journey" that I look back on now, there are things I wish I'd known, skills I wish I'd had, a worldliness and wisdom I would have loved to have fast-tracked. Some might call it the lessons of life.

When Camila told me about the book she was writing, this book, I immediately thought back to '85 and realised just how valuable it would have been for me. I did eventually go back to university and now look back on the ups and downs of a life I hope has been well lived. But the lessons and learning in this book, especially the support for our wellbeing, the advice that helps us contextualise our hopes, fears, anxieties and self-judgements, would have been such an amazing tool; it would have helped me to affirm, to understand and to cope with my changing world, a world that, for you, is spinning even faster.

Read on, drink it in and remember that even at your most vulnerable, you are not alone.

– **Dr Richard Gerver**,
Educator, Author, Speaker;
Expert on Human Potential 2022

Acknowledgements

In the same way that it takes a village to raise a child, it takes the influence, support, example, patience and love of many people to write a book. "I am because we are", as the Ubuntu philosophy tells us, is very, very true!

I want to thank Daniela for her wisdom and insight while I was writing this book. Dani, you helped me make it more meaningful and inclusive. Your dedication, kindness and passion for what's right are inspirational!

Joe, love of my life, with you, and because of you, I have been able to be where I am and share my passion with others. Thank you for loving me in the very many ways I am and have been.

David, you probably don't realise how much you have helped me throughout this book. Your strength of character and experiences inspired many of its pages, and your unstoppable and contagious love for life and adventure kept me going during the hard days. Thank you, mi Davi.

To my Papo, gracias for your advice and ideas based on your wealth of knowledge and experience and for giving me the strength to keep going no matter what. Your words "fly high, fly far but fly well" always stay with me.

Mamita, he aprendido con tu ejemplo la generosidad y entrega absoluta. Gracias por estar presente siempre en nuestras vidas y dar lo mejor de ti sin medida.

To Esteban and Heather, thank you for all the great discussions on student-centred practice and the knowledge you have shared with me. Most importantly, thank you for showing me with your example what resilience looks like and how to be strong even in the most difficult times (and of course, for Milo, my muse).

To Ongara, Juanita, Daniel, Tetea, Teita, Debbie, Aidan and all my family, thank you for believing in me and for being present even when far away. This pandemic has kept us apart, but only from a distance, never from our hearts!

This book wouldn't have happened without all the students I have supported throughout the 23 years I have worked in education. Each and every one of them has informed my thinking and impacted my understanding of what students need to get ready for university, once they are at university, and as they move onto the "real world". Thank you for allowing me to be part of your life journey. Keep making waves to make the world a better place!

To Susanne Clarke, the other half of Sumila at BU, thank you for rescuing me when I needed it and for changing my life by showing me what is possible. Your kindness and passion for excellence have shaped many pages in this book.

To my esteemed scholars Shirley Brooks, Caroline Ellis-Hill, Les Todres and Richard Gerver thank you for igniting my commitment to humanising education with your example and wisdom.

To my Bournemouth University colleagues thank you for embracing me and giving me a safe space to create, innovate and embed my life's work as we continue our quest to humanise education.

To my editors, Molly Selby and Rhea Gupta, thank you for your patience and kindness and for always being available to answer my many questions. It's been a joy to work with you!

To you, the reader, thank you for choosing this book. I wrote it from my heart with the dream that it inspires you to live your best life with authenticity and self-love. I hope it gives you the knowledge and the tools you need to navigate adversity and embrace the joy, to flourish and thrive in this chaotic yet wonderful world.

– **Dr Camila Devis-Rozental,**
September 28, 2022,
Poole, England

1 Introduction

Preparing for your learning journey

▶ WHAT'S THIS BOOK ABOUT?

Hello, reader, I am glad you picked up this book. By doing so, you have joined forces with me on my quest to humanise education, in this case by improving your wellbeing to learn better.

In this book you will find tools and ideas to support you in improving your wellbeing whilst you prepare for the next steps in your life journey. It may be that you are getting ready to go to college, university or find a job. The idea is that in this book, you will learn about the impact that your wellbeing can have on every aspect of your life. I have attempted to make this book as inclusive as possible, and there is no right or wrong way to use it. You can go straight to the chapters that interest you and do the activities that work for you.

If you are an educator wanting to support students in their journey to wellbeing, you can use the activities in this book to engage and empower students as you embed wellbeing within your curriculum.

In this chapter, I will cover:

- The main organisation of the book
- Why I have included trigger warnings

DOI: 10.4324/9781003317548-1

- A little of my story so you understand why I wrote this book
- An overview of the realities of going to university

Although I believe that when thinking about wellbeing, we should do it in a holistic way (looking at ourselves as a whole) as indeed we are, I wanted to break down different aspects of wellbeing and explore them in more depth. Consequently, after a lot of research, I have identified six main dimensions or areas which should be considered when thinking about our next steps. These are:

1. Physical wellbeing
2. Socio-emotional wellbeing
3. Intellectual wellbeing
4. Environmental wellbeing
5. Occupational wellbeing
6. Financial wellbeing

▶ ORGANISATION OF THE BOOK

I will explore these dimensions of wellbeing in detail within the book by covering each of them in their own chapter. For those of you interested in the science of wellbeing (as I am), within each chapter, I have explored the dimension, considering current research and its rationale for taking it into account. One of the great things we know from research is that learning new things gives you more confidence (Devis-Rozental 2018). Additionally, knowing why you are doing something helps you put it into practice and stick with it. So, I would recommend you read these sections as these will give you some great reasons for doing the activities and incorporating new habits into your life.

In Chapter 2, which looks at the dimensions of wellbeing, I define wellbeing and explore the dimensions of wellbeing. I introduce you to some core theoretical frameworks that you can apply to every chapter to help you on your journey to wellbeing. This chapter has an interesting activity for you to reflect on your dimensions of wellbeing.

Chapter 3 covers physical wellbeing, considering various areas with an inclusive approach. I have explored things such as sleep, diet, exercise and other topics that can impact your wellbeing. There is some sensitive content/possible trauma triggers in this chapter around sexual health and substance abuse, so read it with caution; but if you feel it could be triggering, don't read it. It could be a good way to start setting the boundaries to help you on your journey to wellbeing.

In Chapter 4, which is a large chapter, I look at socio-emotional wellbeing with an emphasis on developing strategies that can help you increase your socio-emotional intelligence and develop your self-awareness.

Chapter 5, intellectual wellbeing, is also a large chapter divided in two parts. The first part looks at how you learn, considering intelligence, memory and developing a positive mindset, amongst other things. The second part explores the academic skills you will probably need at university and how to develop them. I cover practical things such as the type of assignments you may have to do.

In Chapter 6, I explore environmental wellbeing, considering three aspects. The first one is how your environment impacts your wellbeing. The second one is how your actions and behaviours impact others, and the third one looks at how you can make a positive impact on your environment with practical ideas.

Chapter 7 looks at occupational wellbeing and introduces you to a variety of activities to find your values and character strengths, and how to apply them to find your purpose. I explore in this chapter the importance of creativity and introduce you to useful models and tools to help you live your best life.

At the beginning and end of each chapter, I have included bullet points with an overview of what is covered in each chapter so you can navigate it with ease.

There are some common themes in each chapter, a type of golden thread that binds them all together, based on the science of wellbeing. These are positive psychology strategies, humanising notions (Devis-Rozental and Clarke 2020), strength-based ideas, learning theories and practical guidance. I have included these as they clearly influence wellbeing as something key to thriving. Once I have explained each of the sections, looking at the current research and theories, each chapter will tell you why the dimension is important for you, how it can help you with your studies/planning and finally, it will include tips, strategies and reflections for you to practice so you can strengthen each dimension. Each chapter has activities for you to complete so you learn about yourself and improve your wellbeing.

▶ CONTENT WARNINGS

In some chapters, you will see that I have added content warnings as I will be discussing sensitive subjects that might be triggering to some people. If you think a topic may upset you or trigger something from previous trauma and you don't feel safe, or it isn't for you, don't read it; that is fine. The main point of this book is to enhance your wellbeing, and the core of that is doing what you feel is right for you.

If you read something that triggers you, make sure you seek support. I have included details of places where you can get specific support depending on which area I am covering. Be kind to yourself; that is also a key aspect of wellbeing.

▶ A LITTLE OF ME TO SHARE WITH YOU

I wrote this book because I feel passionate about wellbeing and how it affects our learning and developing. I have experienced this first-hand, and I think lived experience and storytelling are powerful ways to learn from each other. You may already know about me and my unwavering optimism and love for life if you follow me on Twitter with my handle #ChangingTheWorldWithASmile. Let me tell you a little bit about myself, and you will then understand why I am so passionate about positivity and wellbeing.

I am a disabled academic. I wasn't always disabled; this is something that happened to me when I was at university. I decided to attend university in the UK as a mature student, which was already hard given that I originally come from Colombia, in South America, and English is my second language. In 2005, whilst completing my degree in Education, I had an allergic reaction to a medication that damaged my nervous system and left me unable to do anything at all. I went from being an active individual working as a preschool teacher, studying and raising my children, to suddenly being completely dependent on my husband to do anything at all. I couldn't walk or exert myself due to severe pain, twitches, tremors and violent involuntary movements. My nervous system was damaged – forever.

I lost my independence and, with that, my sense of self. It was a very difficult time that coincided with my completing my degree. As I had to spend time in the hospital and I was unable to go anywhere, I thought I would have to give up. However, with support from the programme leader, my family and friends, I was able to finish my dissertation and graduate on time, albeit in a wheelchair and not feeling myself. This reminded me of how important other people are to support us when we need it, so throughout this book, I will remind you many times that if you need help – ask.

Unable to do my previous job but still wanting to make a difference in education, I started a postgraduate diploma looking at teaching teachers how to teach. So, once I had learned to be okay with having walking aids to help me function, I started the course and began teaching part-time. I was surprised at how much I loved it and how naturally it came to me. I had found my element, that place where I was fully submerged in what I did and loving it (if you want to find out more about finding your element, you can check Chapter 7).

During this time, I had to learn to love myself again and to accept who I was. I had two small children, and I wanted them to learn to never give up on what they wanted to achieve, even if that meant changing plans. It was a difficult journey, and it was never linear. However, it really helped me to discover, as part of my studies, the notions of socio-emotional intelligence and positivity for wellbeing. Learning about myself and how to use the science of wellbeing to help me feel better about myself, and to be able to function, was key to my recovery. Not recovery from being disabled, as that will never change and I am okay with that, but recovery from hating who I had become to loving myself and to reframing my purpose in life. To being okay with using my wheelchair whilst I teach, and to sometimes twitching when I am tired. To finding the collateral beauty, the great things we learn about ourselves or the things that we appreciate even in the painful days.

I can honestly say that I now love and respect myself more than I ever have. I am happy with who I am and to be the way I am. Throughout this journey, I learned that I am strong, resilient and adaptable to change. I have learned that through self-kindness and self-compassion, I am able to listen to my body; that through laughter, I can manage my pain (it never goes away, but I can tolerate it better); and that by learning about myself, I know better what I want and how to do it.

This is something that took years of discipline, effort and commitment. Developing wellbeing is not immediate; it is built over time, and as many people have told me throughout my journey, there is no magic wand, so I decided to create my own road map to finding my happy place, even without a magic wand. I practice daily activities purposefully to improve my wellbeing and maintain my mental health. Of course, I have bad days, and I cry; it isn't like I am happy and cheery all the time; that is not realistic at all. But on the bad days, I allow myself to feel what I am feeling, with the knowledge that these are passing feelings and that better times will come as nothing stands still. I continue to practice all my strategies, and, for me, this has worked, but as I said, over time.

Every single one of us will have a different journey to achieving wellbeing, and that's okay, but if we don't know how to do it, it may sometimes seem impossible. For me, learning about the science of wellbeing and applying it to my own experience has been transformative, and that is why I feel so strongly about sharing it with you. There may be things in this book that you may not find useful or helpful, and that's okay, but I do hope you find some things that resonate with you and your experiences to become the best version of yourself.

▶ WHY HAVE I WRITTEN THIS BOOK?

I have written this book because I am passionate about supporting students to thrive and flourish, but I am aware that this can sometimes be hard if people don't have the knowledge or tools to do it. If we are well, we will do well, so it is important to take the time to take care of ourselves and to make sure we feel healthy, valued, safe and able to be our best selves. I am also on a journey to humanise education, and part of that means to embed wellbeing as part of any curriculum seeing students as holistic beings and wanting them to thrive. This can only be possible with a whole school approach, and this book provides the underpinning theory and practical activities that can be shared in the classroom to support students to flourish (Quinlan and Hone 2020).

Covid-19 stopped our normal way of being, and with this, it affected many aspects of our lives. As we learn to live alongside Covid, we have had to reflect on our boundaries or social activities and the way in which we do everyday things. Lockdown brought isolation, and the lack of human contact affected how we develop relationships. Healing from Covid and the way in which it changed our lives will take time, and the effects of Covid in areas such as education will last for years. It may be that you had to study online and were not able to share important milestones with your friends and family. I had students who had to spend both lockdowns on their own, and that was hard for their mental health. Even though we were lucky to have technology to help us stay in contact and, to some extent, develop relationships remotely, students reported feeling lonely, unable to make friends and finding it hard to motivate themselves.

However, even before Covid, students' wellbeing had been identified as an area that needed further development. In my practice over many years, I noticed that students arrived at university lacking the skills that would help them thrive. Areas such as motivation, resilience or confidence were missing, as well as practical life skills important for university such as organisational skills, study skills, cooking and others. I have attempted to cover these and many more areas within this book.

So there are two further reasons why I have specifically written this book for those preparing for college/university. The first one is because I work with students at university. I know that sometimes students start university unprepared for the experience and that being unprepared and having unrealistic expectations of what being at university can be damaging to their wellbeing. Going to university is a major change in anyone's life. It is a time of rupture from the familiar to something new and, for some of you, an experience where you will have to start from scratch to make new friends, live in a new city and even speak a new language. At university, you will be a self-directed learner, which basically means that you will be accountable to yourself for how and when you learn. You will have long "free" periods where you can use your time however you like, but if you are not organised, this can affect your learning, wellbeing and results.

The second reason is based on research that evidences that knowledge gives us confidence. By learning about yourself and the things that you can do to improve your wellbeing, with a commitment to applying them, you can improve your university experience, learn better and ultimately thrive.

Throughout this book, when I am focusing on going to university or college, I will refer to it as going to university for simplicity, but this book is also for you if you haven't thought about university or if you are about to start work. Basically, if you have finished your compulsory education and are moving on to further studies, whichever these are, this book is for you. Most of the theory and activities that I have included are for personal development regardless of where you are. If you are not moving on to education but rather employment or are going through a change in your life and want to improve your wellbeing, most of the activities in this book will also be useful for you.

▶ THE REALITIES ABOUT GOING TO UNIVERSITY

If you have started to think about going to university, you may already be bombarded with prospectuses, booklets and invitations to visit different places. You may also have started visiting universities where you will be shown the most amazing resources, campuses and activities. There is a lot of competition between universities to get students, and although, of course, there are requirements and some may be very strict, they will want to woo you so that you choose their university. So, when making your decision, make sure you pay attention to how you feel when you are there and that they have the type of support you may need.

Unlike what you may have seen on television, university can be hard, and adapting to it takes time. Of course, you will meet new people and have new experiences, but you will also have to study hard, manage your time and money, and if you move away from home, you may feel lonely or homesick. If you're worried or scared about this, planning for it and getting ready for the difficult parts as well as the amazing ones can really help ease your fears.

You may be surprised to know that most students starting university will feel a mixture of excitement and worry, and that's normal. Everyone will want to make new friends, try new experiences and learn new things. What most people won't share is that they are anxious about being able to make friends, worried about not knowing enough or overwhelmed by all the new things happening at once. In a study conducted a few years ago, we found that students felt an array of emotions after their first week, as you can see in Figure 1.1

Within this book, I have aimed to cover all the areas I know from my research that will be helpful for you to get ready for university

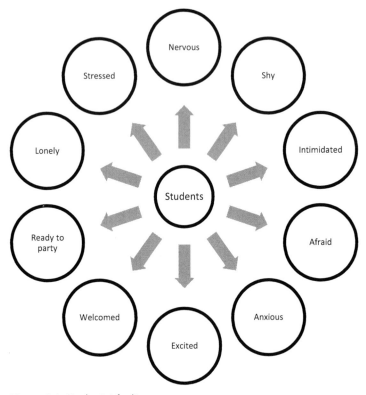

Figure 1.1 Students' feelings

and, once you are there, to flourish. Remember, this is your journey, and how it goes is up to you; you will get back as much as you put in, which goes for every aspect, from making friends to studying and learning new skills.

▶ OKAY, LET'S DO THIS!

So, now you know the "why" of this book and the way in which I have organised it. In the following chapters, you will learn the "how" of how to improve your wellbeing in each of the six dimensions. Some of the activities and ideas may not work for you, and that's absolutely fine; after all, we are all different and learn and develop in different, equally valid ways. The important thing is that you identify those that work, and you practice them. I hope you are as excited as I am to start this journey with you. Remember, be kind to yourself, and have fun as you learn about yourself and improve your wellbeing.

▶ REFERENCES

Devis-Rozental, C. (2018). *Developing socio-emotional intelligence in higher education scholars.* London: Palgrave Macmillan.
Devis-Rozental, C. and Clarke, S. (2020). *Humanising higher education. A positive approach to enhancing wellbeing.* Cham: Springer.
Quinlan, D. M. and Hone, L. (2020). *The educators' guide to whole-school wellbeing: A practical guide to getting started, best-practice process and effective implementation.* Abingdon, Oxon: Routledge.

The foundations of wellbeing

▶ INTRODUCTION

In this chapter, I will explore wellbeing and the areas I consider its foundations; those things that will help you ground it and centre it so that it becomes an essential part of your lived experience. Being well means doing well, so it is important that you look at wellbeing not as a commodity but as a necessity. In order to achieve lasting wellbeing, we first need to understand how that can happen. So, in this chapter, I am going to explore the following themes to kickstart your journey:

- A definition of wellbeing
- An introduction to the six dimensions of wellbeing
- An exploration of nature and nurture
- How your brain can be powerful in enhancing your wellbeing
- Why theory matters and how you should apply it to your experience
- Maslow's hierarchy and how it applies to you
- The importance of focusing on what you can control
- An exploration and application of the tourist metaphor

DOI: 10.4324/9781003317548-2

▶ WHAT IS WELLBEING?

"Wellbeing can be understood as how people feel and how they function, both on a personal and a social level, and how they evaluate their lives as a whole" (New Economics Foundation 2012). Basically, it is how you judge the way you feel, considering all areas of your life. It is about being and feeling as healthy possible, but also about how content you feel with your life; how satisfied and engaged you feel about what you do and how in control you feel you are of your life. There are many factors that can affect your wellbeing. Some will be external and others internal.

Here is a table so you can identify some of these within your own experience:

TABLE 2.1 Factors affecting your wellbeing

External factors	Internal factors
• Where we live	• Psychological needs
• Physical health	• Attachments
• Environmental issues	• Stress
• Access to health care	• Sensory needs
• Finances	• Sense of purpose
• Family	• Beliefs
• Social connections	• Level of education
• Socio-economic status	• Trauma
• Equity, diversity and inclusion	• Sense of identity
• Politics	• Emotions
• Education opportunities	• Mindset
• What we eat	• Habits
• Disability	• Self-esteem
• Sleep	• Confidence
• Time management	• Neurochemistry
• Exercise	• Hormones
• Substance abuse	• The way we think about ourselves
• Change	• The way we see ourselves

As you can see, many things can affect our wellbeing; some of them we can control, whilst others we can't. Thinking about all of these can be overwhelming, and this, in turn, can impact our wellbeing. There are theorists and ideas that have explored this, and learning about them can help us identify which areas we should be thinking about to ensure we are well. So, in the next section, I am going to introduce you to them. You may have heard of some of them, whilst others maybe not, as they have traditionally looked at other subjects that I believe relate to wellbeing. Learning about their ideas has helped me prioritise areas of my wellbeing. One of the things I have attempted throughout the book is to bring you "abundance" ideas instead of "deficit" ideas. By this, I mean that I have looked at the things that work based on appreciation, positivity, growth and flourishing rather than looking at why things don't work and how bad things can get. In my experience, looking at the glass half full is in itself a way to begin the journey to wellbeing – but I will explain more of this later.

▶ SIX DIMENSIONS OF WELLBEING

There are many ways to look at wellbeing, and many authors have looked at the different areas in different ways. I have chosen these six dimensions of wellbeing as the main areas explored within this book:

1. Physical wellbeing
2. Socio-emotional wellbeing
3. Intellectual wellbeing
4. Environmental wellbeing
5. Occupational wellbeing
6. Financial wellbeing

I chose these six dimensions based on students' needs and extensive research. I will define and explore each of these in the chapters following this one.

Regardless of which wellbeing dimension you are interested in exploring, there are certain boundaries which you should consider to help you on your journey of improving your wellbeing. These are:

- Physical boundaries by protecting your personal space
- Socio-emotional boundaries by protecting who you spend your time with and by taking time for yourself when you need it
- Verbal boundaries by protecting how you speak about yourself and the things you talk about
- Time boundaries by protecting how you spend your time
- Financial boundaries by protecting how you spend your money
- Safety boundaries by ensuring you are safe and well
- Work boundaries by making sure you have a balance within your workload and slot time for rest, relaxation and fun things to do

Wellbeing is "contagious" (Quinlan and Hone 2020), so if you are on your journey to improving your wellbeing, you may influence others around you, that will be great for you, and also for them. Sharing wellbeing with others can be a great way to create social bonds with healthy boundaries and a positive outlook. Going to college/university is a big change. There will be many things you have to consider before you arrive and once you are there. Being prepared will help you reduce stress and improve your wellbeing.

To support you with this, I am including the tourist metaphor which I created a few years ago. Hopefully, it will be useful to keep you organised and ready to thrive at university and beyond. Each of these areas has its own specific ideas, activities and exercises; the idea is that you reflect on them as you are getting ready for your next move.

Before we start, it would be interesting for you to map yourself within these areas to see how you see yourself doing in them. You can use the Juggling Wellbeing exercise to place the juggling balls at your current level of understanding or practicing against each dimension of wellbeing from one being the least balanced to six being the most balanced.

Here is an example:

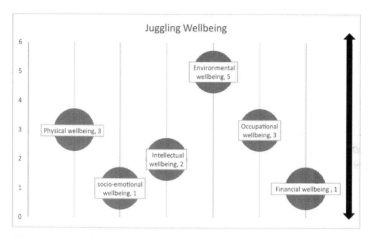

Figure 2.1 Juggling wellbeing example

As you can see in Figure 2.1, the person completing this exercise placed the juggling balls for the six dimensions where they thought their level of understanding and practice of each area was. The arrow on the right-hand side illustrates how the juggling balls can go either up or down. Ideally, as you learn about wellbeing in this book, your juggling balls will go higher.

Activity

Use the blank template below to place your juggling balls where you think you are at this stage. Keep checking regularly to see if you feel they have moved. There will be times where they may go down, and that is okay. Life has its ups and downs, and as you will learn in this book, it is how you approach them that will have an impact on you.

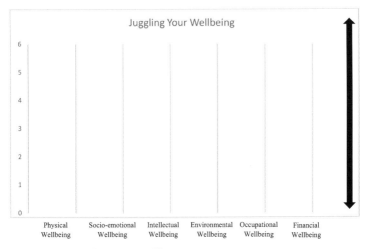

Figure 2.2 Juggling your wellbeing

▶ NATURE AND NURTURE

You have probably come across this debate before. It is one of the oldest philosophical debates in psychology. Even now, some branches of psychology don't fully agree and take on one or the other. For instance, behavioural psychology tends to focus on the impact that our environment (nurture) can have on our behaviour or wellbeing. So if they were looking at stress, they would be thinking about the things that could make us stressed from an external point of view (our friendships, our work, our family life). In contrast, neuroscientists and those interested in biological psychology may look at the genes we are born with and the biological influences such as hormones, body chemistry and others which could make us stressed.

More recently, researchers have moved from looking at nature and nurture as rivals and have started exploring their interaction and how both influence our behaviour and how we develop. For example, an interesting study by Moulton (2014), looking at perfect pitch (an ability to detect the pitch of a musical tone without any point of reference), found that having perfect pitch runs in families; basically that if your parents have it, you are likely to have it too. They were able to single out one gene which could be linked to it. However, even if someone has the gene, it doesn't mean they will definitely develop this ability. For it to develop, there must be opportunities to practice and train in early childhood so that this inherited ability can be nurtured.

This is important to know because it means we are not destined to be a certain way. For example, it means that even if we have a gene that makes us more propense to getting diabetes, we may be able to avoid getting it through the way we eat and exercise. This is not the same for all diseases; some are hereditary, and this cannot be changed. If this applies to you, you will probably already know about it. However, for those which are not fixed, knowing we can do something about it can be a powerful tool to motivate us.

Activity

Make a list of your talents, qualities and physical characteristics. Once you have done that, place each of them where you believe they should be in this diagram:

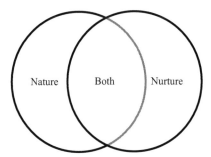

Figure 2.3 Nature, nurture and you

▶ BRAIN POWER

Your brain is a three-pound organ that controls most of your functions. It is therefore a key player when talking about wellbeing. For example, it plays a major role in and is sometimes the protagonist of:

- The way you move
- What you think
- How you learn
- What you remember

- That you see
- What you smell
- What you hear
- What you feel
- How you feel
- Your breathing
- Your heart rate

And many more. Basically, your brain is very powerful and needs a lot of energy to function well, which we will discuss in Chapter 2. It also needs to work out in order to keep functioning well. Although in the past, scientists thought that our brain was fixed and we, therefore, could not change our level of intelligence, our memory, how we learn or what we think, contemporary neuroscientists have discovered that this is not the case. Modern advancements in technology have allowed scientists to look at the brain like never before and evidence that change and growth in the brain are possible.

We now know that our brain keeps developing well into our 20s, and neurons can keep changing by developing new connections throughout our life. This is called neuroplasticity, and it is great news for us as it shows that by exercising our brain, we can actually change it.

Neuroplasticity is the amazing ability that the brain has to change, reorganise and adapt its structure and function as a response to our experiences and activities. This can be good or bad depending on the situation and how we actually use our brain. This can happen without us even knowing, which is why we should build healthy habits to help our brain change positively. Basically, our brain rewires itself by developing new neural connections over time, and these changes, which happen at a structural, chemical and functional level, influence the way we feel, think and act. The more we practice an activity or habit, the stronger the new connection becomes, much like a muscle which is exercised. So why is this exciting? Well, because it means we can influence over time the way our brain works and how to keep it as healthy as possible. There are two main types of neuroplasticity:

- Functional: our brain's ability to move functions from one part of the brain to another, normally from a damaged part to a healthy part
- Structural: our brain's ability to change its structure when we learn something

In this book, we will focus mostly on structural neuroplasticity.

Now, the "over time" statement I wrote above is important, especially when talking about wellbeing. To create a habit and stick to it, you will need to make simple and sustainable behaviours/changes that are realistic (Gardner et al. 2012). This takes time, discipline and sometimes effort. However, the benefits can be great.

Here are some examples of how different activities can impact on our brain:

- We can improve our cognitive skills by playing brain games (memory, focus)
- Learning a new language increases brain density (Pliatsikas et al. 2017)
- Travelling
- Mindfulness meditation improves attention, emotion regulation and even our memory by increasing gray matter (Hölzel et al. 2011)

We will cover these in more depth in the following chapters. So, now we know that our brain can change, but what things do we have to consider for our brain to create these new powerful connections that can increase our wellbeing?

1. Repetition is key. Doing something once will not have a long-term effect, so remember to be consistent.
2. It will take time. You will not feel the changes straight away, so remember to be patient.
3. Challenging our brain. Learning new things or difficult things is key for our brain to change, so remember to keep learning.
4. Focusing on the task. Paying close attention to what we are doing without interruptions or distractions will have more impact, so remember to be focused.

5. Sleepyheads. Sleeping plays an important role in neuron growth, so remember to have a bedtime routine to sleep well.

A note of caution

Even though our brain can change, it doesn't mean every part of the brain at any time can change. Some parts of the brain, such as those involved in movement, speech or in some cases cognition, cannot recover once damaged. And, even if other parts of the body try to make up for it, they may not be able to replicate the functions that have been damaged.

Another important thing to take into account when looking after your brain is how certain substances can affect your brain and change it, but not for the better. Certain psychoactive substances and other chemicals can have a negative effect on your brain long term. I discuss this in more depth in Chapter 3.

▶ THEORY MATTERS

Here are some of the theories and ideas that have motivated me to improve my wellbeing; I hope you find them interesting and useful. Keep in mind that we are all different, and what works for one person may not work for another, so feel free to pick and choose those that say something to you and can be related to your experiences. Before we begin this journey together, there are some overarching ideas that I want to share with you so you can learn about them and apply them to the activities in each of the chapters. These can be powerful tools to get us thinking about what's important and how to lead better lives. In the following sections, I will explain some of these.

▶ PRIORITISING OUR NEEDS: MASLOW'S HIERARCHY OF NEEDS

Abraham Maslow (1908–1970) was an American psychologist interested in theories around motivation. He is mostly known for developing a hierarchy of needs, which is a motivational theory looking at the type of needs we have to fulfil in order to survive and thrive, usually depicted as a pyramid, although Maslow himself didn't design it that way. The needs are organised in a hierarchical manner with the very basic needs taking priority. The order of the needs is flexible based on our own experience, life circumstances and the things we prefer. Maslow's (1943, 1987) hierarchy can be

TABLE 2.2 Maslow's hierarchy of needs

Deficiency needs are those we need to survive and are based on us lacking something.	Within these needs, Maslow identified: • Physiological needs: these are the needs that are vital for our survival (nutrition, shelter, clothing, warmth, sleep, air, drink, sex, shelter, clothing) Maslow explained that if these needs are not met, our bodies cannot function properly, and since these are the most important needs, any other need will become secondary until these are met • Safety needs: these are the needs that we need to have control over our lives (social stability, financial security, safety against injury, work security, health) • Love/belonging needs: these are the needs we have to avoid isolation and develop a sense of belonging (friendships, community groups, family relationships, romantic attachments, social connections) • Esteem needs: these are the needs we have to feel valued, appreciated and respected (sense of self, self-esteem, identity, accomplishments)
Growth needs are those that not necessarily stem from lacking something; instead, these are about wanting to develop ourselves. Maslow (1943) originally only posed self-actualisation as a growth need. However, he later added three further areas.	Within growth needs, Maslow (1969, 1987) identified: • Cognitive needs: (curiosity, exploration, knowledge and understanding, a need to find meaning) • Aesthetic needs (appreciation of beauty) • Self-actualisation needs (being able to realise our full potential, being able to become our best selves) • Transcendence needs (looking further than ourselves by finding purpose, serving others, mindfulness and the pursuit of something beyond ourselves (faith, spirituality, etc.)

divided into deficiency needs, in which the first three layers are the very basic needs mostly reliant on external factors, and growth needs which are more focused on our internal life. Within these two categories, there are more specific needs that should be considered The following table depicts Maslow's hierarchy of needs.

Maslow's original work has been criticised, as he didn't fully take into account the reality that in certain contexts, people will meet "higher" needs before meeting "lower" needs. Whilst universal human needs seem to be present regardless of culture, the idea that the lower needs must be fully satisfied before the higher needs can be met is not always true. Power dynamics, socio-cultural differences, gender, ethnicity and other factors will certainly influence how needs are met. I originally come from Bogota, Colombia, a beautiful country with a complex past and where poverty is quite prominent in some parts.

In Colombia, you often see children begging in the streets, and in some areas, people live in very precarious circumstances, yet they develop meaningful relationships, for example. Clearly no one should live in such levels of poverty where this is the case, and everyone should have their very basic needs met to be able to survive and thrive. Still, this does prove that is not so much the order of the needs that matters but rather acknowledging them and knowing how to fulfil them by looking after ourselves as best as we can. Sometimes fulfilling them is out of our control, and this can be very frustrating, for example, if they depend on the current government or an external situation we cannot control.

How can you use Maslow's hierarchy of needs?

This is a useful tool to check on our needs and make sure we are doing our best to meet them. If we are not, we can then reflect on the things we should be doing to meet them more effectively. For example, it may be that you have been lacking energy and overall are feeling unwell. This, in turn, is making you stressed, and you can therefore not concentrate. So looking at Maslow's hierarchy and thinking about the different needs, you identify that you have not been eating well lately. You have been skipping breakfast and sometimes even lunch thinking that a good evening meal will suffice. However, as your body needs energy constantly, the lack of calorific intake over a long period of time will lower your blood sugar and energy levels, and this may make you feel weak and, overall, unwell. Furthermore, when you then get a calorific intake (eating one big meal), your blood sugar will spike, and this may make you feel irritable.

Identifying that your eating habits need reviewing and doing something about it will help you feel better, and this, in turn, can reduce your stress levels and aid concentration. We will cover more in-depth physical wellbeing in the next chapter. The point here is that being aware of your needs and how to satisfy them can help you feel well, thrive and flourish. Self-care is not selfish; it is key to your wellbeing, and this is something that you will read throughout the book.

Activity

Use Maslow's hierarchy of needs to reflect on your own needs and how these should be met.

TABLE 2.3 Meeting your needs

Deficiency needs	What are my needs?	How can I make sure they are met?
Physiological needs		
Safety needs		
Love/belonging needs		
Esteem needs		
Growth needs	What are my needs?	How can I make sure they are met?
Cognitive needs		
Aesthetic needs		
Self-actualisation needs		
Transcendence needs		

▶ FOCUSING ON WHAT WE CAN CONTROL: COVEY'S CIRCLE OF INFLUENCE AND CONCERN

To help you identify the things that you should focus on, I will introduce you to one of the ideas developed by Stephen Covey (1932–2012), an American educator and businessman. Covey created a self-management tool that distinguishes between the things that concern us, those we may care about but cannot control and the things we can influence. He depicted these as circles to help individuals understand better how to use their mental energy more efficiently.

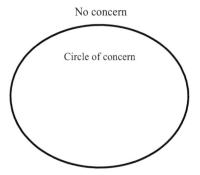

Figure 2.4 Circle of concern

To do this, he identified the circle of concern, which will normally be quite big as it should encompass all the things that worry us regardless of how important these are or if there is something we can do about them. These may be climate change, war, famine, the country's economy or even Covid-19. It can also include things which may seem closer such as the way people perceive us, what people say about us or the way someone talks to us. All these may cause us concern, but we have no control over them. In Covey's idea, if we spend too much time worrying or thinking about these things, we will achieve very little and, in a sense, waste valuable energy. This will make us less productive and efficient.

The circle of influence, in contrast, might be smaller and include things that we may be able to influence but still have no control over, like the impact of your contribution to a team or how someone uses your advice.

In recent years, there has been a third circle added to this model. The circle of control. In this circle you would include the things you can actually do as a result of your choices, your habits, your mindset or your discipline. All the things that you can control such as how you talk to other people, what you watch on television, your social media consumption, how you express your emotions or your habits, etc. To think about these choices, it is important to have self-awareness, to be honest with ourselves and to understand our limitations well. It is also important to want to improve, change or develop. We are sometimes aware of our habits and may want to change them but make little effort. There is no point in buying a subscription to the gym if we never go, for example. Lacking control can be very stressful and damaging in the long term; think about substance abuse, addiction or other self-harming types of behaviour. This doesn't mean that someone who is an addict will be able to change their habits by just identifying them. It will take time, commitment, resilience, perseverance and a support system and in some cases medication for someone to succeed. However, the first step is in wanting to change that harmful habit.

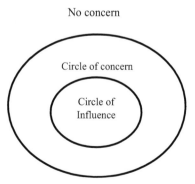

Figure 2.5 Circle of influence

The idea is that if you focus on the things you can control, you will be using your energy for a useful purpose, and this, in turn, may increase your circle of influence. This circle gives you the power to make good choices and the responsibility to follow them through for your wellbeing. Covey believed that we are not the product of our circumstances but of our decisions, making us proactive in the choices we make. I would argue that this is not always the case, as sometimes circumstances do shape who we are. Nevertheless, taking responsibility for our actions and our decisions about those circumstances can be powerful and help us feel in control.

This model can also be applicable to moving on from difficult situations or from worrying too much about the past. Thinking about the past can be good as a reflective tool to see how we can improve ourselves and what we can learn from situations, but it can also hold us back and bring us down if we let it take over our lives. We will discuss this in more depth in Chapter 3 when we are looking at the socio-emotional aspects of wellbeing.

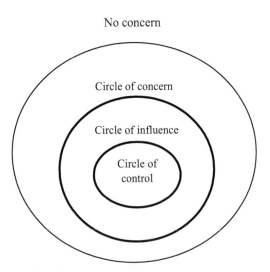

Figure 2.6 Circle of control

So how can you use this model?

This model can be useful for identifying areas to focus on, to look at your priorities and to let go of the things you cannot control. It doesn't mean you should stop your concern for them; it means you should stop worrying about them and concentrate on the things you can control, which could eventually influence them. Covey advocates for someone to be proactive rather than reactive. A proactive person will make attempts to stay focused on the things they can change/improve/control. They take responsibility for their choices and ownership of their decisions. In contrast, a reactive person will spend time and energy on things where they can have little influence; they may procrastinate and feel hopeless. By doing so, their circle of concern will expand. So, you should be proactive and focus on those things which you can change to have a better life.

I have used this model in the past to help me make decisions and even to help me sleep better, and I found it quite liberating. I used to take ages falling asleep because as soon as my head hit the pillow, I would start worrying about all the things I hadn't done. In my head, I would go over and over the same things, passively worrying but without doing anything about it. When I was introduced to this model by a good friend, I decided to use it at night before I went to bed. So in my head, I would make a list of the things that were worrying me. I would then ask myself these questions:

1. Can I do something about this now (as in, immediately)?
2. If yes, I would get on with it and do it
3. If not, and it could be done the next day, I would put it aside for later
4. If not, and I couldn't do anything about it ever, I would, as Elsa said in *Frozen*, let it go

Over time, I found this really helped me to fall asleep quicker and worry less about the things I could not control. Of course, I still care about them, but in order to protect myself, I try not to give them my time and energy.

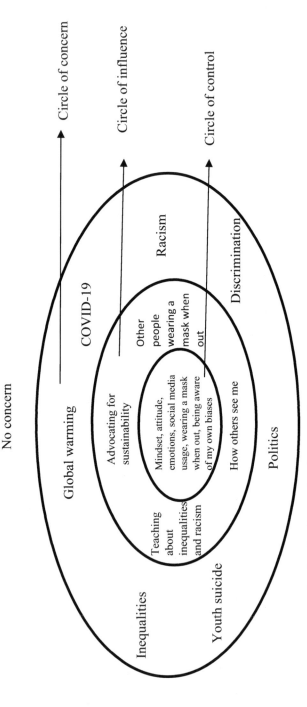

Figure 2.7 Example of circle of control, influence and concern

Here is an example of my circles of control, influence and concern to illustrate how I use them. Yours will be different, and I encourage you to use the blank model to complete your own one.

As you can see in the example above, I have included areas such as Covid-19, global warming and racism as areas I am concerned about. I cannot change those things by myself; however, I may be able to influence them by, for example, teaching about inequalities, advocating for sustainability or encouraging others to wear a mask when out. Those things may have an impact, but I can't control if they do. What I can control is wearing a mask, challenging my own biases and recycling, for example.

Activity

Now that you understand these circles, you can create your own Covey's model to help you identify what you should focus on to get the most out of your experiences and to improve your wellbeing as you slowly stop worrying too much about the things you can't control.

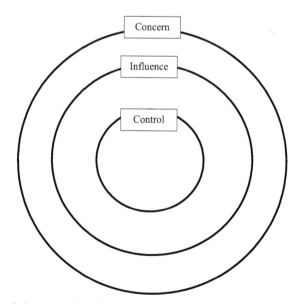

Figure 2.8 Your circles of concern, influence and control

▶ THE TOURIST METAPHOR

Imagine that you are a tourist getting ready for a big trip to a foreign land. In order to get ready to go, you may want to find out as much as you can about this country so you can make the best of it and have an amazing time. Here are some of the things you may want to know before you go:

- Where you are going
- How to get there
- What language do people speak there?
- What currency do they use?
- What is the accommodation like?
- Who can you contact if you need any help?
- Where are the best restaurants/bars/clubs?
- What are the customs there?
- What should you pack?

If you are an adventurer, you may have many other questions. The point is you would want to be prepared to have the best time. What if you looked at going to university or moving on to a new opportunity like that? A new and exciting opportunity where you have to be prepared. To help you do this, I developed the tourist metaphor (Devis-Rozental 2018, 2020). I am not saying that going to university is like a foreign trip, but if you imagine your chosen university as a foreign country, you may be curious enough to want to know how to thrive there. The tourist metaphor identifies a variety of areas which have been labelled as things you would need to know for your trip to get you to reflect on what you would need to get ready for university. As a metaphor, I have used a word or phrase that would normally be associated with travelling to then explore the more specific areas that you may want to investigate before you arrive to university.

For example, in visa requirements, I have included the type of things you would need to be accepted into the university. It doesn't literally mean you need a visa (unless you are an international student, in which case you should case the requirements). Equally, under laws, I mean metaphorical laws which refer to policies and procedures, and if you don't follow them, it won't mean you are breaking the law, but it may mean you are not following the university's rules.

In Table 2.4, I have identified some areas you may want to investigate. Not all will be applicable to you, but it is a good start to get you planning and getting ready.

TABLE 2.4 Getting ready for university by applying the tourist metaphor

Visa requirements (entry requirements)	• Grades needed • Personal statement • Interview • Portfolio • Police checks • Mode of attendance • Specific requirements
Laws (Policies and procedures)	• Policies • Academic integrity • Academic offenses • Rules and regulations • Understanding plagiarism • Student charter
Currency (marking/grading)	• Marking criteria • Marking culture • Referencing • Level of marks • Type of assignments • Feedback • Minimum requirements
Welfare (seeking help)	• Additional learning needs • Wellbeing support • Student services • Sports • Doctor surgery • Equity • Diversity • Inclusion
Time zone (managing time and activities)	• Induction period • Timetables • Self-management • Self-directed motivation • Planning for early or late lectures • Managing free time • Deadlines

Table 2.4 (continued)

Geography (places and spaces)	• Campus location • Building location • Lecture room location • Accommodation • Names of buildings • Online resources • Library and other important resource centres
Culture (social life)	• Student union • Clubs and societies • Higher education culture • Digital presence • Etiquette • Social norms • Freshers' activities • Traditions
Language (academic language/jargon)	• Academic language • Academic skills • Learning outcomes • English as a second language • Regional accents • Communication skills
Economy (cost of living etc)	• Student loans • Student grants • Scholarships • Budgeting • Finding part-time work

Universities will have open days either online or in person that you can attend and where you can ask as many questions as you like so you are ready for your learning journey. One size doesn't fit all, and not all universities will be the perfect fit for you whilst others might, so it is important that you don't rush your decision and choose the university that is best for you considering your needs, skills, hopes and expectations.

For example, you may prefer a smaller university because you don't feel comfortable in very big places, or you may choose to stay in your local university and live at home. Regardless of reputation, league tables or any other predictor, the most important thing is for you to feel that you are going to a place where you can be yourself, study something which fulfils you and where you will be able to thrive.

When you are making your decision, you will have to consider where you will live and how you will pay for things. You should explore how far is your accommodation from university, for example. If you have a disability, you should ensure the university has the tools to support you, that areas are accessible for your needs and that your accommodation is suitable for you and your needs.

Activity

Use Table 2.5 to help you prepare for your own learning journey

TABLE 2.5 Preparing for your learning journey

Visa requirements (entry
requirements)

Laws
(Policies and procedures)

Currency
(marking/grading)

Welfare
(seeking help)

Time zone
(managing time and activities)

Geography
(places and spaces)

Culture
(social life)

Language
(academic language/jargon)

Economy
(cost of living etc)

▶ OVERVIEW

In this chapter, I have explored the notion of wellbeing and the many aspects you need to consider as you embark on your learning journey at university and your commitment to improve your wellbeing. The main areas I explored were:

- A definition of wellbeing so that you can understand what it is and how it links to your own experience
- An introduction to the six dimensions of wellbeing so you can get an idea of what will be covered in the rest of this book
- An exploration of nature and nurture, as these are both important when we are thinking about our wellbeing
- How your brain can be powerful to enhance your wellbeing
- Why theory matters and how you should apply it to your experience as you begin your journey to enhance your wellbeing
- Maslow's hierarchy and how it applies to you
- The importance of focusing on what you can control
- An exploration and application of the tourist metaphor to enable you to think about all the practicalities you will have to consider as you prepare for your next steps

I hope you have found this chapter useful and that as you complete the activities I have included, you have a clearer idea of what you need, what you want and how to do it. In the following chapters, I will explore each of the six dimensions of wellbeing in depth with activities, reflections and theory to help you gain an understanding of what each dimension is and how to improve it.

▶ REFERENCE LIST

Covey, S. (1989). *The 7 habits of highly effective people: Powerful lessons in personal change.* New York: Simon and Schuster.

Devis-Rozental, C. (2018). *Developing socio-emotional intelligence in higher education scholars.* London: Palgrave.

Devis-Rozental, C. (2020). *Socio-emotional intelligence: A humanising approach to enhance wellbeing in higher education.* Cham: Springer. 15–34.

Gardner, B., Lally, P., and Wardle, J. (2012). Making health habitual: The psychology of 'habit-formation' and general practice. *The British Journal of General Practice: The Journal of the Royal College of General Practitioners*, 62(605), 664–666.

Hölzel, B. K., Carmody, J., Vangel, M., Congleton, C., Yerramsetti, S. M., Gard, T., and Lazar, S. W. (2011). Mindfulness practice leads to increases in regional brain gray matter density. *Psychiatry Research*, 191(1), 36–43.

Maslow, A. H. (1943). A theory of human motivation. *Psychological Review*, 50(4), 370–396.

Maslow, A. H. (1962). *Toward a psychology of being*. Princeton: D. Van Nostrand.

Maslow, A. H. (1969). Toward a humanistic biology. *American Psychologist*, 24, 724–735.

Maslow, A. H. (1987). *Motivation and personality*. 3rd ed. New York: Harper and Row.

Moulton, C. (2014). Perfect pitch reconsidered. *Clin Med*, 14(5), 517–519.

New Economics Foundation. (2012). *Measuring wellbeing: A guide for practitioners*. London: New Economics Foundation.

Pliatsikas, C., DeLuca, V., Moschopoulou, E., and Saddy, J. D. (2017). Immersive bilingualism reshapes the core of the brain. *Brain Structure & Function*, 222(4), 1785–1795.

Quinlan, D. M. and Hone, L. (2020). *The educators' guide to whole-school wellbeing: A practical guide to getting started, best-practice process and effective implementation*. Abingdon, Oxon: Routledge.

Physical wellbeing

Taking care of our bodies

CONTENT WARNING

This chapter explores areas that might be triggering to some people, including eating habits, sexual abuse and substance abuse. Please make sure you seek support if you need it and practice self-care.

▶ INTRODUCTION

In this chapter, I will explore key aspects of physical wellbeing, and how these can affect our health, with an emphasis on helping you prepare and thrive during your university experience. At the beginning of the chapter, I will focus on students who may have a disability as there will be additional areas they will need to consider. I would encourage you to read this section even if you don't consider yourself to have a disability as it also includes areas that you may find useful.

Within the chapter, I will explore these areas:

- The importance of staying healthy
- The importance of keeping active, considering your level of fitness

DOI: 10.4324/9781003317548-3

- The importance of eating well and its impact on our body
- The importance of personal hygiene and its effect on our body
- The importance of sleeping well and ideas for how to do it
- The importance of reducing stress and ideas for how to do it
- The importance of being well informed about sexual health
- The importance of avoiding substance abuse

As in previous chapters, you will find tips and activities that you can complete to support you in getting ready for university and to develop your self-efficacy and independence. But before we begin, it is important to understand the meaning of physical wellbeing.

Physical wellbeing is the ability to keep healthy life choices and behaviours that will make you feel good and give you a good quality of life. It's more than having good health as it requires you to make an active effort to ensure you maintain it through daily choices. Taking care of your body is important at university to stay healthy, happy and to maximise your student experience.

For example, a study by El Ansari and Stock (2010) found that there is a clear link between physical wellbeing and academic performance. Basically, if you are well, you will do well. Things like what you eat and drink, how much exercise you do or how much you sleep will have a direct impact on how your brain works and your level of energy, attention and even ability to focus. These, in turn, will have an effect on your studies and your results. In the following sections, I will cover these in more depth. You may have physical wellbeing even if you have a disability; however, having a disability can have an impact on the choices you make and indeed your decision and opportunity to go to university. Therefore, the first part of this chapter explores disability within the context of physical wellbeing and going to university.

▶ DISABILITY AND GOING TO UNIVERSITY

According to the UK Equality Act (2010), you are considered disabled if "you have a physical or mental impairment that has a 'substantial' and 'long-term' negative effect on your ability to do normal daily activities". Having a disability may mean that you must consider where you can study and the things you will need to be able to do it. Consequently, it is key that you do your research about what type of support universities offer, such as the campus and living situation and transport needs, for example. It may be that you received support when you were at school or college, but the type of support and how to access it at university may be different.

You may be surprised to find out that mental health conditions and learning difficulties are also considered disabilities, and even though you may not feel comfortable calling yourself disabled, getting the right type of support can make a great difference to your university experience. So don't feel worried, embarrassed or scared to disclose your situation. It will only benefit you in the long term.

In fact, setting up the support you will need takes time, so it is important that you start planning early for your life at university. Some universities require you to register for support before you arrive at university, while others will ask you to do it after. Registering is very important as it can give you access to reasonable adjustments, funding and support. It is up to you if you declare your disability, no one can make you do it; however, I encourage you to do so as it can save you a lot of time and provide you with many benefits to help you succeed.

I have a physical disability. I became disabled whilst at university, and I can categorically say that without the support from my university and funding from disability student allowance, I would not have been able to finish my studies successfully. There are certain things you will need to consider regarding the university you choose. You can check these out when you go to an open day. Open days are a great opportunity to get a feel for the university but also to ask staff and students any questions you may have about the university. I would encourage you to make a list of the things you want to find out so that you get all the answers you need.

Activity

You can use this table as a prompt to make sure you ask useful questions when you visit a university

TABLE 3.1   University support available

University support	How can I contact them?	How can they support me?
Academic support available		
Learning resources		
Learning environment (disabled accessible)		
Online platform (how inclusive is it?)		
Living accommodation		
Campus accessibility		
Mental health support		
Student services		
Student union		
Student groups and societies		

In the UK, when you are completing your student loan application, there is a separate form to complete to be able to receive DSA (Disabled Students' Allowance). This is a non-means-tested allowance given to every disabled student who applies and can demonstrate through evidence from their doctors that they have a disability. The type of support can vary greatly. Some people get special equipment, discounts on disabled accessible accommodation, a support worker, a notetaker, money for transport and other types of things depending on your specific needs. For instance, students with dyslexia, ADHD (attention deficit hyperactivity disorder) or OCD (obsessive compulsive disorder) may get extra time to complete their assignments or during exams. The type of support you may get is completely personalised and will be based on your needs.

Here are the main things you need to consider if you have a disability and need to get some support:

- It is your responsibility as an adult to seek the information you need and apply on time
- You should apply for DSA before you start your programme
- You must be able to provide evidence such as a letter with your diagnosis, and in some cases, they may want to speak to your doctor
- You may need to register with your university's disability service
- You will need to attend a needs assessment so that you can get what you need (this may take some time, so it's important to apply early)
- The support you will need will be fully funded by DSA if you are eligible. If you are not, you should still speak to the university disability services about alternative funding options

▶ STAYING HEALTHY

Keeping well at university will help you do better and feel good. This can sometimes be difficult if you are not taking care of your basic needs. However, your health must always be your priority, so if you feel unwell in any way, you must make sure you get some help. There are some things that we can do to stay healthy, and in the next sections, I cover some of them. Ensuring you bring with you the medicines you normally take (if you take any), registering with the local GP practice (doctor surgery) and understanding your body so you know what is good for you are all key aspects.

We are all individuals, and what works for you may not work for someone else, so take this into account when looking through this section. Additionally, there are things which you may not be able to control, such as getting a cold or "freshers' flu" as it is sometimes called. However, what you do and how you do it may influence how well you recover and your chances of getting it.

It may be that you have to take medicine regularly, and there will be times where you might become unwell. So for those times, I have created a list of items that you may need to take with you to university.

Activity

Use this table to make sure your first aid kit has everything you need to look after your health.

We all come in different shapes and sizes

Every body is different based on our genetic and our environment. Our frame, bone structure, weight, size and shape are all unique to us. Even if we all ate the same thing every day and

TABLE 3.2 First aid kit checklist

First aid kit
Any medicines you would normally take
Antiseptic wipes/cream
Thermometer
Plasters (make sure to find out if you are allergic)
Cotton wool
Cotton buds
Pain reliever
Hot water bottle
Heat pack
Cold and flu medicine (make sure you seek advice before taking any medicine)
Dressing for larger wounds
Adhesive tape (check for allergies)
Disposable gloves (check for allergies)
Scissors

exercised the same amount, we would still look different. The ideal body doesn't really exist, and trying to achieve it at any cost can be dangerous for our health. Weight fluctuates, and two people may weigh the same and look completely different depending on how much muscle or fat they have, alongside the other factors I just mentioned. Sometimes you may feel pressured to look a certain way.

I struggled with my body image most of my life, mostly because when I was growing up, I was bullied and called fat quite a lot. I was brought up in a society where people saw being skinny as being beautiful and where this was much more important than being healthy. Looking back, I wasn't fat. I had a large frame, and even at my slimmest, when I was hungry all the time (which is not healthy), I still saw myself as fat. This distorted body image was hard to shift to be able to love myself as I am. The funny thing is that now that I am older and quite large due to my disability, I love myself more than ever, and I am happy to be who I am. This took many years of practicing some of the many things I have shared with you in this book. This is not to say that if you feel you have to lose or gain weight because of your health and wellbeing, you shouldn't do it. But what is the ideal weight?

According to NEDA (2022), "your 'ideal' body weight is the weight that allows you to feel strong and energetic and lets you lead a healthy, normal life". So focusing on keeping as active as you can, whilst listening to your body and eating well for your health and wellbeing, are much more important than attempting to change your body to look a certain way or how others look.

▶ KEEPING ACTIVE

Introducing physical activities to our daily routine can be great for our wellbeing. Some people think that if they prioritise their bodies, go to the gym, go for a walk or do some exercise, they will be wasting time or feel as if they are doing less work. In fact, taking care of your body will make you more productive and help you produce better work. These activities may give you time to think and reflect on what you have been learning and therefore cement it in your memory.

We are all different, and the level, intensity or type of exercise you do will depend on your ability, level of fitness as well as your capability or limitations. The main thing if you are able is for you to keep active on a daily basis. The recommended amount of exercise for an adult is about 30 minutes per day, and this can be broken into small chunks or done in one go. You need to find what works for you.

Here are some of the benefits of keeping active every day:

- Better concentration and memory
  When you exercise, blood and oxygen flow to your brain as well as release important proteins, and this makes your neurons very active, particularly in your hippocampus, which is the part of the brain that helps process and retrieve information.
- Better mood
  When you exercise, especially doing high-intensity exercise such as running, aerobics or Zumba, your endorphins (feel-good hormones) are released into your body. This can help you feel good, more relaxed and can make your brain work more efficiently. Research shows that low-intensity exercise such as yoga or Pilates can help reduce anxiety and depression (Stanton and Strock 2014).
- More energy
  It may sound strange, but energy boosting exercises such as running, cycling, walking, and going to the gym, when practiced regularly and consistently, can be great to fight tiredness as they increase energy levels. However, you must consider your level of fitness, and if you have a medical condition that prevents you from exercising, you must consult with your doctor and always listen to your body
- More creativity
  Yes! If you want to be more creative, you should engage in regular exercise. A study by Colzato et al. (2013) found that exercise affects divergent thinking (the way your mind generates new original ideas or solutions).

It is important to remember that overexerting yourself and doing too much exercise can be counterproductive and, in extreme cases, dangerous, so it is key that you be sensible, listen to your body, and if you have a disability or health condition that prevents you from doing exercise, please contact your doctor before starting any type of exercise.

Activities to stay active

You may find that these activities, whilst not purposeful exercise, can help you stay active.

- Walk more (if you are able)
- Fidget whilst doing some work
- Exercise whilst watching TV
- Do some housework

▶ HOW TO RELEASE THOSE FEEL-GOOD HORMONES?

Here are some research-evidenced ways to release the hormones that make you feel good.

Activity

For the goal and reward activity, I want you to set a goal around physical activity. It could be anything big or small that you want to achieve in one week. The important thing here is that you must be small, specific and realistic about what you are able to do. Here is my example to give you an idea.

- My goal this week is: to spend some time outdoors at least three times this week
- I want to do this because: spending time with nature is good for my health
- The thing that could stop me from achieving my goal could be: the weather

TABLE 3.3 Happy hormones

Endorphins (the stress-relieving hormone)	Doing exercise Laughing with friends Hugs Dancing Listening to music
Oxytocin (the love hormone)	Being kind to others Spending time with people you like Kissing and hugging someone you love Meditation Yoga
Serotonin (the happy hormone)	Sunshine Spending time in nature Meditating Listening to music you like Dancing Remembering happy events
Dopamine (the reward hormone)	Sleeping well Finishing the things you start Eating nutritious food Practicing self-care Celebrating successes

- I will make sure I minimise this by: wearing something waterproof
- I will reward myself when I achieve this by: watching my favourite show

Now, you have a go:

- My goal this week is:
- I want to do this because:
- The thing that could stop me from achieving my goal could be:
- I will make sure I minimise this by:
- I will reward myself when I achieve this by:

▶ FOOD, GLORIOUS FOOD

CONTENT WARNING

This section covers areas around healthy eating habits that may trigger some people. If you feel this may affect you, please

don't feel you have to read it, and seek help (www.beateating disorders.org.uk)

Feeding our brain for optimum learning and our body to have the energy it needs to function are also key. Did you know that our brain burns about one fifth of the calories we eat? Research shows that eating well can have an impact on our body and our mind too. In fact, a poor diet can change our brain chemistry, and this can result in anxiety, irritability, low mood and addictive behaviours. At the same time, people who suffer from anxiety and depression may eat a poor diet as part of their symptoms as they are not able to care for themselves properly. If this is the case, it is important to seek help from your doctor.

Eating regularly helps your body regulate your blood as energy is released slowly, and this will help you stay focused. A lot of students who come to university don't have breakfast due to a lack of time or planning. This is not a good idea – leaving a very large gap between your evening meal and your next meal the following day will impact your blood sugar, and this can make you feel unwell. Additionally, it will make you feel tired and lethargic during lectures and seminars and therefore unable to pay attention or even learn.

What you eat is up to you, and of course, coming to university and perhaps living on your own for the first time, it may be tempting to eat junk food. However, the benefits of eating healthy and well are worth a bit of planning and thinking.

The World Health Organization (WHO) recommends that you eat at least five portions of fruits and vegetables a day. The reason for this is that they have lots of nutrients, vitamins, fibre and antioxidants that your body needs to be well. These can be eaten in many ways and from very different sources. A varied diet will have lots of different colours and a range of different types of fruits and vegetables. For more information, you can check the Eat well NHS page which you can access here: www.nhs.uk/live-well/eat-well/

At school, you probably learned about the different food groups (proteins, carbohydrates, fats, grains, dairy/alternative, fruits and vegetables). Our bodies need all of these to some extent. Consequently, diets that avoid a food group (even fats) should be seen with some suspicion as this can be dangerous in the long run. This doesn't mean that being a vegetarian or a vegan is not healthy. The important thing here is to eat the right proteins to substitute the animal products. Additionally, it is important to ensure that those with health conditions follow the appropriate diet to help it manage it.

Protein builds our muscles

Proteins such as fish, eggs, cheese, meats, nuts, beans, lentils and soya products contain amino acids. These are chemicals that help the body break down food and repair, grow and regulate our thoughts, amongst other things. These are, therefore, important for us to consume.

To fat or not to fat

Poor fat has received a lot of bad publicity. The reason for this is that all types of fats have been grouped as one. Although trans and saturated fats can be bad for our health (anything fried, fats in cakes, some processed food and junk food), healthy fats such as monounsaturated and polyunsaturated fats found in healthy oils found in olive oil, avocados, nuts or other foods and omega 3 found in oily fish can be good for our health. These good fats can lower your blood pressure, give your brain some extra energy and protect your heart.

Carbs are good for you (in moderation)

Carbohydrates are your body's main source of energy and contain very important nutrients. They can help you boost your mood and also protect you from getting sick. For example, fibre has been shown to protect you from type 2 diabetes. However, it is important to choose the right type of carbs to help your body function well, especially since carbs become sugar as they enter your body, and too much sugar isn't very good for you.

Sweetie pie

Sugar is the simplest form of carbohydrate, and it occurs naturally in many types of foods. Like everything else, in moderation, sugar is not bad. However, too much sugar is bad for your teeth and your body in general. There are studies that show that sugar can increase inflammation, for example. According to the NHS (2021), adults should only have about 30g max of sugar per day, so it is important to be sensible about how much sugar you consume. This is not to say that you cannot have a piece of cake or a sweet treat occasionally. The key is in ensuring that these yummy treats don't become an everyday thing. And of course, if you have a medical condition that is affected by sugar, you should always follow your doctor's advice.

Water is life

Most of us have heard that we should have between six to eight glasses of water/fluids every day. The reason for this is that our bodies are mostly water (about 70%), as are our brains (again about 70%). Apparently, even a 2% water loss can affect our brain from working well, so hydrating is really important. When you are dehydrated, you will feel more tired and sometimes not able to concentrate. Water is great for our skin and keeps our kidneys working well. Some people don't like water, so drinking other fluids such as juices, squashes, smoothies, tea or coffee (in moderation) also work well.

Happy gut

A healthy diet is key to making sure our digestive system works effectively. Eating enough fibre, fruits and vegetables, as well as whole grains and plenty of water, is a great ways to do so, but did you know that managing stress can also help your gut work well? Well, the gut-brain connection is a real thing. Have you ever felt butterflies in your stomach, or sick when you are nervous? The reason for this is simple. Your digestive system is sensitive to your emotions. When you are stressed, anxious or worried, your brain sends messages to your stomach, and this can have an impact on your toilet habits; it can also give you heartburn or a stomach ache. This, if chronic, can result in developing digestive disorders such as irritable bowel syndrome. Consequently, to keep your stomach "happy", you must eat well but also feel well and reduce stress.

Caffeine

As a stimulant full of antioxidants, coffee will give you a fast burst of energy, which can be useful at times. For example, studies have found that it can make you more alert, have more energy, concentrate better, and it can even help solidify new memories (Evans et al. 2021).

However, drinking too much coffee can have a negative impact on your nervous system, sleeping patterns and even your mood. So, what is the correct amount of caffeine you should have? A study by Rodríguez-Artalejo and López-García (2018) found that drinking one to three cups of coffee per day was tied to a 15% reduced risk of cardiovascular disease. This, of course, will depend on an individual's health. The study warns that this is only recommended for those with well-controlled blood pressure. So, if you suffer from blood pressure issues, you must always consult with your doctor.

Cuppa tea

If you are a tea drinker, you will be happy to know that many studies show that tea can boost your immune system, fight inflammation and even impact your heart (Khan and Mukhtar 2013). This is especially the case for green tea, white tea, some herbal teas (ginger, peppermint, chamomile and others) and black tea too, although black tea is caffeinated, so like with the coffee, you need to drink it in moderation. There are some teas that should be avoided, like very sugary teas, or for those with allergies, herbal teas that could trigger them.

Activity

For this activity, you are going to practice mindful eating. To do this, try to make yourself a balanced meal. Once your food is ready, find a comfortable place where you can eat it without too many distractions.

- Put your food in front of you and look at it, paying attention to what it is and the type of food it is (carbohydrate, sugar, protein, etc.)
- Pay attention to the smell of the food, the colour of the food and its texture
- Now try the food, and pay attention to the taste, texture and sound when you are eating it. Is it soft, hard, crunchy, hot, cold, sweet, savoury, etc.?
- Eat it slowly, and as you eat it, keep paying attention to every bite and savour it
- Once you have finished the food, spend a couple of minutes in silence thinking about what you liked, how the activity made you feel and what could be the benefits of paying attention and taking your time when you eat something

▶ PERSONAL HYGIENE

Taking care of yourself and your body by keeping clean is important, as every day you may come into contact with millions of viruses and germs. Due to Covid-19, now more than ever, there is an awareness of how vital it is to maintain good personal hygiene. Having a grooming routine is beneficial for your health as well as your mind. Your idea of good personal hygiene may be different from others, and this may be due to your upbringing, culture and sometimes what is available to you. For example, some people like a shower in the morning, while others prefer a bath at night. Still there are some basic habits that are almost universal. These are:

- Showering or bathing regularly with soap and water (should ideally be practiced daily, but if you do exercise, you may need to do it more often)
- Drying thoroughly after showering/bathing with a clean towel (should be practiced every time you do it)
- Brushing and flossing teeth (should be practiced at least twice per day)
- Washing hands after using the toilet with soap and water (should be practiced every time you use the toilet). If you are somewhere where there is no running water, you should use a hand sanitiser instead
- Washing hands before eating with soap and water (should be practiced every time you are going to eat)
- Cutting nails on your hands and feet with a nail clipper or nail scissors (should be practiced every couple of weeks depending on how fast your nails grow)
- Washing hair (each person is different, so it is up to you and your type of hair)
- Using hygiene products for menstruation in the correct manner (pads and tampons must be changed according to the given instructions)
- Use sunscreen daily, even if it isn't sunny
- Moisturise your skin daily
- Using a face mask when you are in a crowded place (even if it isn't a requirement anymore, it should be practiced)
- Taking care of your hair (brushing or combing)
- Using deodorant or anti-perspirant daily
- Bedding should be changed once per week
- Face and body towels must be changed at least once per week

Doing these basic things on a regular basis can help prevent infections, body odour, bad breath or dirty hair.

If you use glasses, contact lenses, hearing aids, retainers, patches or other medically required devises, you must make sure you keep them clean and that your hands are clean when you are going to touch them. It is also important to keep them in the right place when you are not using them so they stay clean. For example, keeping a retainer in its special box, or glasses in a pouch.

Maintaining good hygiene can also prevent illnesses such as:

- Tooth decay
- Athlete's foot
- Urinary infections
- Gum problems
- Diarrhoea
- Acne
- Scabies
- Ringworm

There are other routines such as shaving, plucking or waxing hair, having facials, using hair products or body fragrances that are a personal choice and will very much depend on your preferences, your culture, your upbringing and the type of skin or hair you have.

Additionally, taking care of our hygiene is great for our mental wellbeing. In fact, one of the telltale signs of someone who may be having mental health problems is that they may stop showering or brushing their teeth. Being clean will make you feel good.

Keep your clothes clean by washing them regularly. Avoiding using underwear or socks more than once before washing them and not leaving your clothes on the floor are also areas to consider when thinking about personal hygiene. At university, you may not have a personal washing machine or dryer, so it may be that you need to be organised and plan a day in the week for doing your laundry. Make sure you budget for it because using these machines in a launderette, even at university, costs money.

Physical appearance and self-esteem are closely related, and the way you care for your body will have an impact on how you view yourself, so make sure you are kind to yourself by making the time to care for your body. You will feel better for it.

Activity

Here is a checklist to help you identify which things you are taking to university to help you with your personal hygiene. I have left some blank spaces so you can add your own ideas:

TABLE 3.4 Personal hygiene checklist

Personal hygiene survival kit
Face masks
Body wash
Hand wash (soap)
Shampoo
Body towel (2)
Hand towel (2)
Toothbrush
Toothpaste
Floss
Hairbrush
Nail clippers/scissors
Tissues
Face wash
Moisturisers (face and body)
Hand sanitiser
Sun protection

▶ WHEN YOU SLEEP, YOUR BODY RECOVERS

When you sleep, your body is working very hard. It is during this time that your cells recover, your brain makes connections and assimilates information. Lack of sleep is one of the most identified issues that students have when they start university. The new routine, self-managed time and all the activities available makes students poor sleepers (Kabrita et al. 2014). For students, staying awake and pulling an all-nighter can be commonplace. Lack of sleep can have a detrimental effect on your wellbeing, so if you haven't done it, try not to start it. More importantly, if you have a good sleep pattern, try not to break it. Sleep deprivation has been used as a form of torture (Leach 2016).

The quality of our sleep and how much we sleep can be linked to academic performance (Ness and Saksvik-Lehouillier 2018). Sleep can help us memorise, retain information, recall facts, be more creative and learn better. From a physical health point of view, lack of sleep has been linked to obesity, coronary heart disease and diabetes. According to the NHS, these are some benefits of sleeping well:

- Boosts your immune system
- Improves your mental health and wellbeing
- Prevents certain illnesses as mentioned previously
- Increases your sex drive

How much should we sleep?

It seems that between six to nine hours of quality sleep is the average for an adult, but everyone is different, and some people need more sleep than others. For example, babies need a lot of sleep as they are constantly developing. If you feel rested after a good night's sleep, you are probably sleeping the right amount for you. If you sleep well but wake up tired, fatigued or lethargic and can't shake the need to have constant naps, you should consult your doctor. If you have caring commitments, parental responsibilities or if you work late nights, it may be difficult for you to sleep well as this is out of your control. If that's the case, try to be creative in finding moments when you can sleep and recover. For example, if you are a parent, try to sleep when your child is asleep. If you child doesn't sleep much, like one of my children did when they were little and you are suffering from sleep deprivation, ask your doctor or health visitor for some support.

If you know you haven't been sleeping well, make sure you modify your habits and, if necessary, your routine so you get used to sleeping better. It won't happen overnight, but with a routine and consistency, getting optimum sleeping time can be achieved.

Creating an ideal environment for a good night's sleep:

- Have a bedtime routine by trying to go to bed at the same time every day
- Try to minimise the use of electronic devices before you go to bed
- Ensure your room is at the right temperature (16–18 centigrade seems to be the optimum)
- Make sure your PJs are comfortable
- Make sure your bed is clean and not too hot or cold
- Make sure your room is dark enough whilst being comfortable for you
- Reduce noise level if possible
- Ensure your bed, duvet and pillows are comfortable
- Make sure your room is tidy and clean

Once your sleeping environment is right, you need to make sure your mental state is also ready for a good night's sleep. This can be hard if you feel nervous, anxious or if you are an overthinker, as it may be difficult to quieten your mind. Here are some things you can do to help you develop the right mindset for a good night's sleep:

- Try to focus on the things you can control. Think:
  - Can I do something about it now?
    - If yes, go do it
    - If not, let it go. It will still be there tomorrow
- Distract yourself by using your imagination to think of a calming situation or place
- Accept your thoughts as just passing, and let them go instead of fighting them
- Do something that relaxes you before bedtime (stretches, meditation, listening to calm music)
- Avoid the news, social media or any other triggering places before you go to bed

Tip: Sleepstation.org.uk has a wealth of free information and resources to help you sleep better.

Activity

If you are not a very good sleeper, this exercise might help you identify why that is.

- Prepare your sleeping environment considering the ideas presented in the section above
- Spend five days paying attention to your routine before you go to sleep, and make some notes of what works to make you go to sleep and what doesn't
- On the sixth day, see if there are any common things on the days you slept well and the ones you didn't
- If you can identify some activities that helped you sleep, try to incorporate them into your bedtime routine if you can
- If you can identify some activities that didn't help you, try to remove them from your bedtime routine

▶ STRESS AND THE FIGHT OR FLIGHT RESPONSE

The fight or flight response is a reaction that your body has to a perceived stressor. It allows your muscles to react faster to either run away or face a situation, depending on the circumstances. Stress is a natural reaction to something that your body or mind perceives to be a threat, and it can be very helpful as a way to manage difficult situations. It was key to early humans for their survival; faced with a predator, they would either fight or flee as cortisol and other hormones reacted to the situation to keep these prehistoric humans alive.

The problem is that our brains haven't changed much in all the time from your early ancestor to you. So even though our lives are very different and our stressors too, our brains have stayed the same. This means that to our bodies, a threat is a threat regardless of how life-threatening it is. Basically, anything that our body perceives as a threat is a stressor; to our bodies, a crocodile following us, or not having enough money to pay the rent, will have the same biological response, and this can be problematic.

Experiencing stress over a long period of time can be detrimental to our body and overall health. Stress can impact your blood sugar, your blood pressure, your mood, your skin and even your pain tolerance. Therefore, managing stress is key to your physical wellbeing.

Ways of managing stress

- Take a break
- Watch out for signs of burnout such as:
    Feeling tired and drained most of the time
    Doubting yourself all the time
    Feeling overwhelmed and worried all the time
    Feeling very negative about life
    Feeling like everything is too hard to do
    Feeling that you are alone and nobody can help
- Practice self-care
- Listen to your body
- Eat well
- Sleep well

Activity

This activity is called the ABCD (antecedent, behaviour, consequence, distraction), and it is good to identify how we react when we are stressed.

Think of a time you felt really stressed about something and identify:

TABLE 3.5 ABC activity

Antecedent (what happened before you became stressed)
Behaviour (how did you show your stress?)
Consequence (what happened after your response)
Distraction (what could you do to avoid getting stressed next time?)

▶ LET'S TALK ABOUT SEXUAL HEALTH

CONTENT WARNING

This section will cover sensitive areas that some readers may find troubling, including explanations of sexual violence. If you think this might be triggering, please make sure you seek help (https://rapecrisis.org.uk).

A HEPI report by Natzler and Evans (2021) presenting the findings of a survey with over 1000 undergraduate students in the UK exploring sexual health found that many students don't think they've had sufficient sexual health education from their school or their parents. This was especially the case for marginalised groups such as disabled, LGBTQI and ethnic minority students. They also found that students would like to know more about consent before they start university and would also like to have a better understanding of how to have healthier and safer sexual practices, for example, regarding protection or STIs. Therefore, in this part of the chapter, I will explore these themes.

Part of our physical wellbeing is impacted by our sexual health, so it is important that we take it into account. According to the World Health Organization (WHO 2006), sexual health is "a state of physical, emotional, mental and social well-being related to sexuality". It isn't only about illness or dysfunction. It "requires a positive and respectful approach to sexuality and sexual relationships, as well as the possibility of having pleasurable and safe sexual experiences, free of coercion, discrimination and violence. For sexual health to be attained and maintained, the sexual rights of all persons must be respected, protected and fulfilled".

Within this definition, there are some very important points to expand on. The first one is that sexual health influences our holistic wellbeing. Being able to express our sexuality free of stigma and stereotypes while respecting ourselves and others will have an impact on our sense of self. Within the context of physical health, this would mean making sure that we are safe and avoid putting ourselves in situations which may harm us. This is not always possible, of course, but being aware of this can help us gauge situations to stay safe.

The second one is that it isn't just about thinking about sexual diseases but also about the way in which we think and behave towards sexual relationships and sexuality, which, according to WHO (2006), is

> a central aspect of being human throughout life encompasses sex, gender identities and roles, sexual orientation, eroticism, pleasure, intimacy and reproduction. Sexuality is experienced and expressed in thoughts, fantasies, desires, beliefs, attitudes, values, behaviours, practices, roles and relationships. While sexuality can include all of these dimensions, not all of them are always experienced or expressed. Sexuality is influenced by the interaction of biological, psychological, social, economic, political, cultural, legal, historical, religious and spiritual factors.

Clearly within this definition, the holistic aspect of wellbeing is evident when talking about sexuality and sexual health.

The third one is that it acknowledges the importance of ensuring that sexual experiences are free from discrimination, violence or coercion and therefore consented to by all parties involved. This is a key area when talking about sexual health and being safe. In the following section, we are going to explore these in more depth.

Sexual discrimination is when you are treated unfairly because of your sex. Within the context of sexual health, this can include:

- derogatory comments
- inappropriate sexual language
- inappropriate sexually explicit questions
- shouting out inappropriate insults about someone's body
- **Consent** is an agreement between individuals to engage in sexual activities. It must be freely given and can be withdrawn at any time. When someone gives consent, they must not be drunk, drugged or medicated in a way that they are not aware

of what they are agreeing to do, and of course, someone should never engage in sexual activities with an individual who is asleep or unconscious. The age of consent is different in different parts of the world, so if you are unsure, make sure you are fully aware of what it is where you live.

Consent must be given without pressure, bullying or shame. It is important here to remember that it is more than no means no, especially as silence can indicate someone isn't comfortable. It is the presence of a yes that can be withdrawn at any point by any party, and this must be respected.

If you are unsure about what to do, the main thing is to always ask. Some people may say it can be embarrassing or cringey to ask, but if you feel confident enough to kiss or touch someone, you should feel confident enough to ask if it is okay to do so.

Another important aspect to consider is that engaging in sexual activity once doesn't mean it should always be expected. Consent may be:

- Agreeing to a sexual activity by explicitly saying yes
- Letting your partner know that it is okay to stop at anytime
- Checking if something is okay before you do it
- Stopping immediately if you or your partner are uncomfortable
- Listening to you or your partner's concerns and coming to an agreement where both parties have chosen freely
  Someone is not consenting to a sexual activity because they dress in a certain way that may seem sexy or because they flirt.

- **Sexual violence** is any sexual activity that happens without consent, where someone has felt pressured, bullied, intimidated, forced, threatened or manipulated to do something they don't want to do. This includes online activities. Some types of sexual violence are:
  - Rape, which is sexual intercourse without consent. This involves any type of penetration, and it is a crime
  - Sexual assault of any nature, including kissing or groping if it is without consent
  - Sexual trafficking, which is a criminal activity where someone is forced to engage in a commercial sexual activity
  - Stalking, which is the repeated harassing, following or calling someone who doesn't want it in a way that makes them fearful, worried or anxious

- Engaging in any sexual act with a minor
- Spiking a drink to get someone to engage in a sexual act
- Indecent exposure, which is when a person purposefully shows their genitals or masturbates in a public place
- Female genital mutilation, which is when someone's genitals are deliberately cut or injured with no medical reason
- Domestic abuse of a sexual nature, which is when a person of any gender sexually assaults their partner

The main thing to remember is that without consent, any sexual activity is always sexual violence. If someone has been a victim of sexual violence, it is key to acknowledge and believe that it isn't their fault and to seek help as soon as possible. Seeking support will help them deal with what has happened, and it will also be useful to check, for example, in the case of rape, if they may have contracted a sexually transmitted disease or if they could be pregnant.

According to the NHS, these are some places that can offer help in the UK to a victim of sexual violence:

- Sexual referral clinic
- GP (doctor or nurse practitioners)
- The police (dial 101 or, if it is an emergency, 999)
- NHS direct (dial 111)
- Voluntary organisations such as Rape Crisis, Galop, Victim Support, Women's Aid or Male Survivors Partnership, for example

All these charities can be found online.

- **Keeping safe** whilst engaging in sexual activity is something that must always align with your values. Everyone is different, and people from different cultures or religions will have different beliefs, and these must always be respected. You have the right to be treated with respect based on your beliefs and the responsibility to respect others too.

  Learning to respect yourself by being clear about your boundaries with yourself and with others should be the first thing you practice. This will help you avoid being in uncomfortable situations. So if you ever feel uncomfortable, uneasy or don't like how someone is treating you within the context of sexual health, make sure you speak up, leave if you can and report it as soon as possible.
- **Safe sex** is sexual contact in which there is no exchange of vaginal fluids, blood or semen. This can be achieved by always

using a condom correctly, which will dramatically reduce the risk of sexually transmitted infections (STIs) or unwanted pregnancy. Practicing safe sex is especially important if you have sex with someone you don't know very well, or if you engage in sex with more than one partner. If you are in a relationship and you have both been tested and mutually agree, you should be able to have unprotected sex safely. However, educate yourself about the risks and how these could affect you. For example, what would you do if you get pregnant? How would that impact your life? Are you ready to be a parent or to have an abortion? All of these things should be discussed if you are engaging in unprotected sex and pregnancy is a risk.

- **Masturbation** is the self-stimulation of genitals in a sexual way to have an orgasm. It is perfectly normal, providing it is practiced in a private space, without exposing yourself to un-consenting people. Masturbation can be a good way to get to know your body; it is known to reduce stress and anxiety by releasing happy hormones such as dopamine, endorphins and oxytocin. However, if you don't masturbate, that's also okay; it is a completely personal decision, and it could be influenced by your culture, your spiritual beliefs or your lack of interest in sexual activities. Being pressured to do it can leave you feeling guilty, dirty or ashamed, and in this case, it wouldn't be good for you. Ultimately, the choice to do it is yours alone, and whatever you choose is okay, and you should always feel comfortable with your decision.

▶ DRINKING ALCOHOL IN MODERATION

Drinking doesn't have to be part of your university journey. Indeed if you don't drink, you shouldn't feel pressured to do so. According to DrinkAware (2022) "one in six 16- to 24-year-olds in the UK (16%) say they don't drink at all". So you shouldn't feel left out or missing out if drinking doesn't appeal to you or is something you don't do because of your beliefs and values. Make sure you assert your preferences and enjoy the many activities that will be available where drinking isn't included.

If you do drink, you will find that there will be plenty of parties and activities where alcohol will be available. You may have heard of Freshers week, the first week of university with many activities to get you settled at and an opportunity to make friends, join clubs and activities and try new things. During this week, there are normally parties in pubs and clubs where you will have access to alcohol. I am sure you are already aware that drinking too much is bad for your health. It is recommended that you drink less than 14 units a week to avoid health risks and that you don't drink on a regular basis. Drinks, especially alcohol, have quite a few calories, so it can also affect your weight. Drinkwise.co.uk has a handy unit and calorie calculator in their website. This calculator will tell you how many calories and units any drink has, so it is worth checking it out.

If you drink, you are probably aware of how a hangover feels. The headache, fatigue, nausea or vomiting and dehydration are some of the symptoms people get. However, drinking too much can lead to alcohol poisoning, and it can be dangerous, especially if it affects your motor skills or your memory.

This is not to say that you shouldn't drink if you are allowed legally to do so. Whether you drink or not is up to you, but if you do, make sure you keep safe and never coerce someone who doesn't want to drink to do so.

If you are going to drink, DrinkAware (2022) shares some things you can do to keep safe.

1. Know your limits
2. Make sure you eat before going out
3. Try not to drink alcohol before you go out
4. Keep an eye on how much you spend on drinks
5. Drink at your pace
6. Get snacks whilst drinking
7. Hydrate
8. Keep an eye on your friends and stick together
9. Watch your drink

10. Don't accept drinks from a stranger
11. Never drink and drive
12. Make sure taxis and cabs are licensed (keep a phone number at hand)

▶ SUBSTANCE ABUSE

CONTENT WARNING

This section explores substance abuse, which some people may find triggering. If you think it may affect you, please seek help (www.talktofrank.com).

Substance abuse is the overuse of drugs and or alcohol that affects the user significantly. For example, they may start missing lectures, avoiding family or getting into dangerous situations such as driving under the influence. It can include illegal and legal substances.

Some illegal substances in the UK are:

- Cannabis (if not prescribed by a doctor)/marijuana
- Cocaine/crack
- Heroin
- Opium
- Ecstasy
- Ketamine
- LSD
- Methadone
- Crystal meth
- Mushrooms
- Hallucinogens
- Inhalants

The website www.talktofrank.com has a comprehensive A–Z list of drugs. Alcohol in large quantities and overuse of some medicines, such as codeine and other pain medicines, stimulants or some antidepressants, without prescription, although legal, can become an addiction. This is sometimes called substance dependence.

Why do people use drugs?

There are many reasons why people use drugs. It could be due to curiosity or a desire to experiment. It could also be due to peer pressure or because the drugs are not hard to find. Other people may want to use drugs because they like the feeling they have when they take them or because they aren't happy with their lives and see it as a way to escape their realities.

Peer pressure can be quite difficult to manage. This can particularly be the case when starting university and making new friends. It is important that you reflect on where you stand regarding drugs and alcohol and that you stay true to yourself. Here are some ideas on how to do just that:

1. Prepare and practice what you are going to do and say if you feel pressured
2. Be clear and consistent. If it isn't for you, say NO
3. Step away from the situation
4. Think about who is offering you the substance: if they are pressuring you into something you are not comfortable with, they are not really your friend, or they may be so intoxicated that they may need help

If you decide to try something, make sure you know what you are putting in your body and the effects this can have. Whatever the reason, using drugs can be dangerous. It can affect your relationships, impact on your finances and negatively impact on your studies. According to DrugWise (2022), here are some dangerous effects of using drugs:

- LSD, magic mushrooms, cannabis and ecstasy
  - Hallucinogenic effect
  - Affects people's senses

- Can lead to worrying experiences
- Unpredictable behaviour
- Cocaine, crack, ecstasy and other stimulants
  - Induce anxiety
  - Panic attacks
  - Can be dangerous for people with heart problems
- Alcohol, heroin and tranquilisers
  - Sedative effect which can be fatal if taken in large quantities
  - Loss of motor skills, which can cause accidents
  - Physical and mental dependence

Anxiety, panic, drowsiness, breathing difficulties, dehydration and loss of consciousness can happen. Nobody can be certain of how a drug may affect them, even if they have taken it previously. In an emergency, the most important thing is to call an ambulance and be honest about what you or your friends have taken. This can save lives.

▶ KEEPING AS SAFE AS YOU CAN

Any type of drug, either illegal or legal highs, will always have a degree of risk, and you should always understand these risks and how they can affect you or others. I would never advice anybody to use drugs. However, if you decide to use drugs, there are certain things you can do to protect yourself to some extent.

These are:

- Know what you are using and its effects
- Drink plenty of water
- Don't use substances alone; do it with someone you trust
- Make sure you have some money to get you home
- Make sure your phone is charged
- Write down what you have taken and how much in case you pass out
- Try not to mix drugs
- Make sure you use clean equipment
- Make sure you know your way home

If you feel unwell, ask for help. You can find more information about keeping safe here: www.keep-your-head.com/assets/2/drugs_staying-safe1.pdf

▶ THE EMOTIONAL TOLL OF ADDICTION

When someone has an addiction, it will affect every aspect of their lives and that of those around them. It is important not to underestimate how much it can affect someone's sense of self. It may be that they've had to lie constantly to be able to maintain their addiction, and that makes them feel guilty. It can also be that when they are high or drunk, they behave violently, and once they are sober, they regret what they have done. Some of the psychological effects of addiction are:

- Shame and guilt
- Anxiety and depression
- Irritability
- Mood swings

These effects can last long term, even once someone has stopped using. Recovering addicts often feel a deep sense of guilt and shame, and it can be difficult for them to let go of this guilt. Seeking help is the most important step an addict can take. As someone recovers from substance abuse, they should also work on their emotions and mental wellbeing. Part of that will be about forgiving themselves and practicing self-compassion. You can read more about self-compassion in Chapter 4.

Activity

Write a safe card, and keep it with you in case you ever need it. You can write it on your phone for ease. Identify the main things you want to do to be proactive in keeping safe:

TABLE 3.6 Safe card

My emergency contact is:

I live at:

I am allergic to:

▶ OVERVIEW

I hope you have found this chapter useful and informative. I tried to cover all the areas that may have an impact on your physical wellbeing and how they can affect it. Here is a summary of what I have covered:

- A definition of physical wellbeing, because knowledge gives us confidence
- The importance of being well informed about going to university if there are any adjustments or accommodations to be considered
- The importance of staying healthy
- The importance of keeping active, considering your level of fitness
- The importance of eating well and its impact on our body
- The importance of personal hygiene and its effect on our body
- The importance of sleeping well and ideas for how to do it
- The importance of reducing stress and ideas for how to do it
- The importance of being well informed about sexual health
- The importance of avoiding substance abuse

Remember, this is your learning journey, and it is up to you to take ownership of your physical wellbeing and to take care of yourself. If you arrive at university well prepared and, throughout the journey, practice self-care, your experience will be much better, and you will learn more, not only about your degree but also about yourself.

▶ REFERENCE LIST

Colzato, L. S., Szapora, A., Pannekoek, J. N., and Hommel, B. (2013). The impact of physical exercise on convergent and divergent thinking, *Frontiers in Human Neuroscience*, 7(824), 1–6.

DrinkAware.co.uk. (2022). *Freshers week survival guide*. Available from: www.drinkaware.co.uk/advice/staying-safe-while-drinking/freshers-week-survival-guide [Accessed 1 August 2022].

DrugWise. (2022). *Promoting evidence-based information on drugs, alcohol and tobacco*. Available from: www.drugwise.org.uk/[Accessed 10 October 2022].

El Ansari, W. and Stock, C. (2010). Is the health and wellbeing of university students associated with their academic performance? Cross sectional findings from the United Kingdom. *International Journal of Environmental Research Public Health*, 7(2), 509–527.

Equality Act. (2010). *Definition of disability*. Available from: www.legislation.gov.uk/ukpga/2010/15/section/6 [Accessed 11 January 2022].

Evans, J., Richards, J. R., and Battisti, A. S. (2021). *Caffeine*. Treasure Island, FL: StatPearls Publishing.

Kabrita, C. S., Hajjar-Muça, T. A., and Duffy, J. F. (2014). Predictors of poor sleep quality among Lebanese university students: Association between evening typology, lifestyle behaviors, and sleep habits. *Nature and Science of Sleep*, 6, 11–18.

Khan, N. and Mukhtar, H. (2013). Tea and health: Studies in humans. *Current Pharmaceutical Design*, 19(34), 6141–6147.

Leach, J. (2016). Psychological factors in exceptional, extreme and torturous environments. *Extreme Physiology & Medicine*, 5(7).

Natzler, M. and Evans, D. (2021). *Student relationships, sex and sexual health survey*. London: Higher Education Policy Institute, 139.

NEDA. (2022). *Every body is different*. Available from: www.nationaleatingdisorders.org/every-body-different [Accessed 19 October 2022].

Ness, T. E. B. and Saksvik-Lehouillier, I. (2018). The Relationships between life satisfaction and sleep quality, sleep duration and variability of sleep in university students. *Journal of European Psychology Students*, 9(1), 28–39.

NHS. (2021). *Why lack of sleep is bad for your health*. Available from: www.nhs.uk/live-well/sleep-and-tiredness/why-lack-of-sleep-is-bad-for-your-health/ [Accessed 11 March 2022].

Rodríguez-Artalejo, F. and López-García, E. (2018). Coffee consumption and cardiovascular disease: A condensed review of epidemiological evidence and mechanisms. *Journal of Agricultural and Food Chemistry*, 66(21), 5257–5263.

Stanton, R. and Strock, C. (2014). Exercise and the treatment of depression: A review of the exercise program variables. *Journal of Science and Medicine in Sport*, 17(2014), 177–182.

WHO. (2006). *Sexual and reproductive health.* Available from: https://www.who.int/teams/sexual-and-reproductive-health-and-research/key-areas-of-work/sexual-health/defining-sexual-health [Accessed 25 January 2023].

Socio-emotional wellbeing

Happy me, happy you

CONTENT WARNING

This chapter explores topics that might be triggering to some people, including mental illness, self-harm and suicide. Please make sure you seek support if you need it and practice self-care.

▶ INTRODUCTION

In this chapter, I will explore the importance of socio-emotional wellbeing to support you in your studies. There has been a rise in mental health issues, which have been exacerbated by the Covid-19 pandemic. Having the knowledge and awareness of how our happiness can impact our overall wellbeing, considering our socio-emotional health, is therefore very important. In this chapter, I will first define socio-emotional wellbeing and explore mental wellness so you can understand how it differs from mental illness. I will then explore socio-emotional intelligence (SEI) and go through its main areas with a focus on how these can affect university life.

DOI: 10.4324/9781003317548-4

Within the chapter, I will provide a series of evidence-based ideas, strategies and exercises to help you improve your socio-emotional wellbeing and thrive at university and beyond.

The main areas I will cover are:

- Understanding socio-emotional wellbeing
- Defining socio-emotional intelligence
- Exploring self-awareness
- Exploring motivation
- Exploring managing emotions
- Exploring self-compassion
- Exploring empathy
- Exploring social awareness

▶ SOCIO-EMOTIONAL WELLBEING

Socio-emotional wellbeing is a mental state where we feel stable and content with our emotions and the way we perceive the world around us, considering our social interactions (Bericat 2014). This is based on subjective and objective measures. The subjective measures are the judgements we make about the extent to which we feel content, happy and secure within our life. The objective measures are those measurable statistics developed externally to measure quality of life. These could include social progress, economic performance, unemployment and others. Both measures influence our socio-emotional wellbeing and should be considered.

Socio-emotional wellbeing is a key aspect to consider when preparing to go to university. Research has shown that socio-emotional wellbeing is linked to academic achievement (Berger et al. 2011; Devis-Rozental 2018).

▶ MENTAL WELLNESS

Mental wellness is the active process of strengthening our mental, socio-emotional and psychological states by learning how to do it and applying this knowledge to our daily life.

It can help you learn and deal with stressful situations and to cope better as you learn more about yourself and what works for you. Mental wellness will help you thrive and flourish and therefore live a better life. In Chapter 2, I discussed Maslow's hierarchy of needs; mental wellness will help you self-actualise as you pursue self-fulfilment and happiness.

According to the World Health Organization (WHO 2014), mental health is a "state of wellbeing where a person has the ability to cope with everyday stressors, work productively, contribute to their community and fulfil their potential".

Understanding your emotions and how you feel or behave is important, as this can affect your ability to learn and make the most of your time at university. For example, feeling sad is not the same as being depressed, and understanding these distinctions makes easier to know when to seek support and the type of support you may need.

▶ MENTAL HEALTH LITERACY

In order to really be able to develop our own mental wellness, it is important to understand and know how to use the best words to describe various components of mental health and wellbeing. Mental health literacy can really help us to unpick the differences between sadness and depression, fear and anxiety or moodiness and bipolar disorder. Everyone experiences mental health, and with that can often come mental distress. But some of us will experience mental illness, and understanding the differences between these terms is key to understanding the best ways to seek help and to help yourself overcome these challenges.

According to Mental Health Literacy (2022), understanding the difference between mental distress, mental health problems and mental illnesses/disorders, which are known as mental health states, is "crucial to getting the right kind of help if needed, to avoid seeking treatment when it is not needed and to be clear about the language we use to tell others how we are feeling". If you want to learn more about the mental health states and work on your mental health literacy, go to www.mentalhealthliteracy.org.

These are the main mental health states which I've adapted from the online tool I developed for students:

TABLE 4.1 Mental health states

Type of mental health state	What it means	Examples	Type of support
No distress	Ability to adapt to changes and to manage difficult situation effectively. Being self-aware and able to identify how you feel and managing those feelings and emotions effectively is part of mental wellness.	Feeling positive, motivated, engaged or energised	No intervention needed, remember to practice self-care
Mental distress	A range of stressful feelings and emotions you may experience when faced with difficult situations. These are a normal part of our human experience and can also have an impact on our physical health. These are transitory, which means they will pass and can be managed by building resilience.	Feeling sad, disappointed, unhappy, annoyed, angry, anxious for a short period of time	Make sure you have a support system to help you get through these periods, and work on building your resilience. If things seem to be getting worse, seek professional support
Mental health problem	Mental states that may happen when you are dealing with much larger stressors than our usual experience. These can affect your cognitive abilities, your behaviour and impact on your everyday tasks.	Grief, despair, lack of motivation, constant state of stress or anxiety Feeling demoralised	If these challenges are causing you distress or affecting your everyday activities, it is vital that you seek help from your GP or mental health services in your area. Asking for help is the first step, sometimes the hardest but the best you can take to your way back to health
Mental disorder/ illness	Medical conditions that significantly and persistently challenge your emotions, behaviours and wellbeing. These may need to be diagnosed by a health professional and will likely need intervention.	Depression, anxiety, bipolar disorder, eating disorders, panic disorders and other serious conditions	You may already be receiving support from a health professional. If you aren't but you feel you may be suffering from a mental illness, you must seek support. In some cases, you will need medication to help you manage a condition

Activity

Think about the way you feel, how you see yourself, and how you manage your emotions, and try to identify where you consider yourself to be within the mental states table.

• I think my mental health state is:
• Based on my mental health state, I am aware that I need to:

You may find it useful to complete the socio-emotional intelligence questionnaire in the next section to help you learn more about yourself.

If you identify that you may need mental health support, please make sure you seek it. A good place to start is by contacting your doctor, but you can also check out the charity www.mind.org.uk, which supports people in crisis.

Self-harm

Self-harm is when someone hurts themselves to cope with their feelings, memories or overwhelming situations (Mind 2020). Sometimes people self-harm, and they don't know the reason why they are doing it. When someone self-harms, they may feel a release in the short term. However, the reason they may be self-harming hasn't disappeared, so self-harming might become a habit. People who self-harm can also feel embarrassed, ashamed or disgusted after they do it.

According to Mind (2020), there are many ways in which people self-harm, so sometimes it may be difficult to know if you are self-harming or not. If you are concerned and would like clarity or information, visit www.mind.org.uk, where you can find resources to help you through this. It can be triggering or distressing to read explicit information about self-harm, so please ensure that you are in a safe space and mindset to be able to engage with this information, and if you feel you are not, please seek further help, as outlined later in this chapter.

If you or someone you know self-harms, it is important to seek support in the right place. Speaking to a health professional, calling a support line or checking out a mental health charity are ways to get the appropriate support. While using the internet and social media to reach out to trusted organisations, such as www. mind.org.uk, seeking help through social media can potentially be harmful. For example, trying to reach a celebrity or influencer for support or affirmation: they may be unable to answer everyone, and you might feel disappointed, frustrated or upset when you don't hear back from them.

Suicide

Suicide is when someone intentionally ends their own life. There are many reasons why people attempt suicide. Mental illness, depression, substance abuse or even physical health can be reasons why someone dies by suicide. People who feel suicidal have thoughts about dying or spend time thinking about how to kill themselves. Feeling suicidal comes in many forms. Some people feel unable to cope, others feel hopeless, in terrible pain, useless or desperate without a way out. Saying or thinking things like: "the world would be better off without me", "I am a burden" or "I don't want to be in this world" and other self-loathing things are examples of the type of things people may believe when they feel suicidal.

Isolation, poor sleep, change in appetite, inability to communicate, neglecting to take care of one's needs may be signs of depression, anxiety or suicidal feelings. This is not to say that everyone that feels like this sometimes is suicidal, but these feelings can escalate without the proper support.

If you or someone you know is feeling suicidal, it is important to seek help in the right place. By this, I mean contacting your doctor, a charity or a helpline or speaking to a family member or a trusted friend. As I mentioned before, social media can be harmful, and trying to seek reassurance or help there can be dangerous if it is not in the right place. One thing that helps me manage my social media usage is to follow accounts that look for the good in life and promote positivity, kindness and compassion.

There are support groups online that can also be helpful, but if you are going to join them, make sure you check that they are legitimate and well moderated.

If you don't have someone around that you feel you can talk to, here are some places in the UK that can help someone in distress without judgement:

- Call 999 in the UK
- Call Samaritans 116 123 for free
- www.mind.org.uk
- SANEline 0300 304 7000
- National suicide prevention helpline 0800 689 5652

One way to take care of our socio-emotional wellbeing is to learn about it and practice strategies that help us become more self-aware. This is where socio-emotional intelligence comes in.

▶ SOCIO-EMOTIONAL INTELLIGENCE

Socio-emotional intelligence (SEI) is a term I developed considering areas around emotional intelligence, social intelligence, practical wisdom and wellbeing. SEI can be defined as:

> the ability to integrate feeling, intuition and cognition to acknowledge, understand, manage, apply and express our emotions and social interactions . . . Its overall aim is to have a positive impact on our environment and to engage ourselves and others to be present, authentic and open; in order to achieve a sense of wellbeing and to build effective relationships in every aspect of our lives.
>
> (Devis-Rozental 2018, p. 1)

This definition is different from others as it considers the impact we can have on those around us and our environment and therefore isn't an egocentric definition that only looks inwards for personal benefit. It is also distinct because it considers our intuition, which is our ability to pick up something without reasoning.

Intuition is that gut feeling we sometimes get without apparent reason, where our body seems to be giving us cues signalling to something we can't quite understand. According to scientists, these feelings are the result of certain processes happening in your brain. Without us even noticing, our brains are constantly working, predicting situations based on our previous experiences and memories to be ready for action and to keep us safe (van Mulukom 2022). This happens subconsciously whilst our analytical thinking, which I discuss in the intellectual wellbeing chapter, is a conscious act.

This doesn't mean that every time we have a gut feeling, we must follow it, as sometimes the signals from our brain may be heightened by anxiety or just plain wrong. However, it does mean that when we get a gut feeling, an uneasy feeling when something is happening, instead of ignoring it, we should stop and look for cues around us to try to understand what our brain is trying to tell us. Paying attention to your intuition and curiously engaging with it is important to gauge if it may be cognitive bias or anxiety. This curiosity can help us decide if we should follow it or not and can help us actively work through our own biases and unlearn them.

The fascinating thing is that cognition and intuition complement each other and can work together if we use them often. Like everything else discussed within this book, practice and consistency can have a positive effect on our wellbeing. In this case, by fine-tuning the way we think and feel. The main thing here is not to overthink a situation but to listen to our bodies, feelings and emotions and then act.

Areas of socio-emotional intelligence

After years of investigating SEI, I have divided it into six areas (see Figure 4.1).

The most important is self-awareness, as learning and knowing about ourselves will help us identify and develop the other areas.

Activity

Before I explore each of the areas in depth, you can complete the socio-emotional intelligence questionnaire I have adapted from one of my previous books (Devis-Rozental 2020). This is not a psychometric test and should only be used as guidance to help you identify which areas of socio-emotional intelligence you have as strengths and which need further development. It is important for you to remember that we are all different and that this questionnaire is only designed to prompt you to reflect on your SEI and to allow you to think about which areas you feel you would like to work on. So, if you get a low score in any of the areas, try not to worry, as this is only a guidance, and see it as an opportunity to learn about the area/s to improve your experiences.

Figure 4.1 Areas of socio-emotional intelligence

Instructions:

1. Complete the SEI questionnaire by scoring each statement from 1 ("This is not me at all".) to 5 ("This is *so* me".)

TABLE 4.2 SEI questionnaire 2

SEI questionnaire

Question	Points 1–5
1. I know when I feel angry	
2. I find it easy to understand how my friends feel	
3. I can easily motivate myself	
4. I know when I am stressed	
5. I am able to understand other people's behaviour	
6. I am good at meeting deadlines	
7. I am good at working in teams	
8. I feel good about myself	
9. I don't find emotions overwhelming	
10. I always know when my friends are sad	
11. I really like who I am	
12. I don't like to leave things to the last minute	
13. I know when to stop myself from doing something that isn't good for me	
14. I know how to calm down when I am upset	
15. When my friends are sad, I feel sad too	
16. I know when I feel emotional	
17. I love making other people feel better	
18. I can calm myself down easily	

SEI questionnaire

Question	Points 1–5
19. I am easy to get along with	
20. I don't need other people to praise me to feel good about myself	
21. I never procrastinate	
22. I never get angry	
23. I thrive on meeting my deadlines	
24. I can make friends quite easily	
25. I think positively about myself	
26. I can easily see things from my friend's point of view	
27. I can easily identify my strengths	
28. I know what makes me happy	
29. I know how to behave in different situations	
30. I don't let difficult situations affect me much	

2. Now place your scores against each question:

TABLE 4.3 SEI scoring (adapted from Devis-Rozental 2020, p. 26)

A. Self-awareness	B. Motivation	C. Managing your emotions	D. Self-compassion	E. Social awareness	F. Empathy
Q. 1	Q. 3	Q. 9	Q. 8	Q. 5	Q. 2
Q. 4	Q. 6	Q. 14	Q. 11	Q. 7	Q. 10
Q. 13	Q. 12	Q. 18	Q. 20	Q. 19	Q. 15
Q. 16	Q. 21	Q. 22	Q. 25	Q. 24	Q. 17
Q. 28	Q. 23	Q. 30	Q. 27	Q. 29	Q. 26
total	total	total	total	total	Total

You can evaluate your score in the following way:

TABLE 4.4 Analysing your results (Devis-Rozental 2020, p. 27)

5–12 points	This area of SEI requires some attention as a developmental need
13–18 points	Continue building this area of SEI
19–25 points	This area of SEI is one of my strengths

Now record each area according to answers, and identify possible ways to continue developing it:

TABLE 4.5 Recording your results and personal development plan (Devis-Rozental 2020, p. 27)

Area	Needs attention	Continue developing	Strength	How can I strengthen this area?
Self-awareness				
Motivation				
Managing emotions				
Self-compassion				
Social awareness				
Empathy				

Now that you have identified which areas of SEI are your strengths and which need a bit of development, let's look at them in more depth.

▶ SELF-AWARENESS

"Self-awareness is our ability to understand how we feel and how we behave in different situations. It is also about knowing our strengths and weaknesses and how to develop them or improve them" (Devis-Rozental 2020, p. 19).

TABLE 4.6 Self-awareness archetypes by Eurich (2018)

	Low external self-awareness	High external self-awareness
High internal self-awareness	**Introspectors** People in this group know who they are but don't challenge their views by feedback from others.	**Aware** People in this group know who they are, what they want and how to accomplish it. They seek and value feedback from others.
Low internal self-awareness	**Seekers** People in this group still don't know who they are or what they stand for. They may get frustrated with relationships.	**Pleasers** People in this group focus on appearing a certain way to others and tend to overlook what matters to them.

Being able to understand ourselves better has many benefits. More self-aware people tend to be better at communicating; they are also often more creative and have stronger relationships. According to Eurich (2018), there are two types of self-awareness: internal and external. In her work exploring self-awareness and leadership, Eurich identified four self-awareness archetypes mapped within the external and internal realms.

I think we are never one of those in isolation; depending on our circumstances, our relationships, the type of situation and even our mood, we may be able to identify ourselves with one of those archetypes.

Activity

Where would you put yourself in the table above at this very moment?

How can we develop our self-awareness?

- Looking through a window
- A Johari window (Luft and Ingham 1955) is a technique designed to help you understand yourself better by reflecting

on four different areas with the help of someone that knows you well and can give you honest feedback.

- The areas are:
  - Open area: what is known by you and is also known by others.
  - In this area, you should include the attitudes, behaviours, emotions, values and feelings that everyone can see in you and you can see in yourself.
  - Blind area: what is unknown to you but others know about you.
  - In this area, you would ask your friend to give you feedback about how they see you.
  - Hidden area: what you know about yourself but others do not know.
  - In this area, you should include the things you feel you don't need to share with others. It could be things like your fears, goals or dreams; it is up to you.
  - Unknown area: what you don't know about yourself and is also unknown by others.
  - This is the most difficult area to identify because neither you nor your friends know them. However, it is the most exciting one because they are the things you discover along your learning journey, perhaps by talking to your friend or reflecting on your experiences. This area may be easier to reflect on once you have explored the other three areas.
  - The Johari window can be a very useful tool to really learn about yourself. You can see the window in the following figure:

	What I know about me	What I don't know about me
What others know about me	1 Open area	2 Blind area
What others don't know about me	3 Hidden area	4 unknown area

Figure 4.2 Johari window

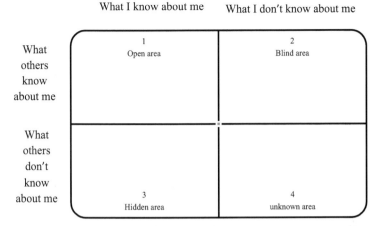

Figure 4.3 Working on your Johari window

- Now that you know about the Johari window, why don't you have a go? Here is a blank window for you to fill.
- Note your goals and priorities
- Reflect and ask yourself: look back at situations where things have/have not worked well and learn from them
- Practice mindfulness: pay attention to the present moment to acknowledge, without judgement, how we feel and why at a particular moment (Devis-Rozental 2018)

▶ MOTIVATION

Motivation means "to be moved by something" (Ryan and Deci 2000, p. 54). It is the way in which we use our deepest feelings and emotions to get us to where we want. There are intrinsic (internal) and extrinsic (external) motivations, and these are unique to us depending on our preferences, circumstances and situations.

Intrinsic motivation is when you do something because you enjoy it, because it makes you feel good or because it is interesting. Conversely, extrinsic motivation is doing something that will give you an external reward. For example, it could be money, a prize or good grades.

Both types of motivations play an important role in learning. Wanting to learn in to improve ourselves and to get good marks are both good reasons. However, an overemphasis on extrinsic motivators can be counterproductive because the rewarding feeling from getting the extrinsic motivator is short-lived, whereas the internal feelings we get from achieving something are more long-lasting. Of course, this is very much dependent on individual circumstances. Some people have no choice but to work more to have enough money to survive.

Things that can influence your motivation

These are some of the different things that can influence how motivated you are to do something:

- Your level of ability (how easy or difficult you find something)
- Your level of curiosity (how interested you are in doing it)
- Your level of autonomy (how able you are to do it by yourself)
- Your values, goals and beliefs (how much you want to achieve something or what it means to you to be able to do it)

Activity

Think about something that you feel very motivated about, and write next to each statement a sentence about it.

Now that you have done that, reflect on how you would apply these ideas to something that doesn't motivate you.

TABLE 4.7 Reflection on motivation

Your level of ability
Your level of curiosity
Your level of autonomy
Your values, goals and beliefs

What can help you motivate yourself?

There will be times during university or at work where you will find activities boring and, therefore, difficult to motivate yourself. Here are some ideas that you can practice to feel more energised and motivated.

- Remembering your goal
  Having your goal in mind can be a powerful way to motivate yourself. Keep visualising the goal and how it will make you feel to achieve it.
- Developing healthy habits
  Any of the activities in this book will help you develop healthy habits to motivate you. Find the ones that work for you, and practice them with enthusiasm and with a positive mindset.
- Being realistic
  This is really important as it will help you manage your time and your expectations.
- Practising self-kindness
  Giving yourself the time to do an activity but also the time to rest, eat and even to do something fun can help you develop self-kindness. Remember, perfection is overrated. If you try your hardest, that's good enough.
- Being clear about what you want by asking yourself:
  - Can I do it?
  - Am I interested?
  - Do I have control over it?
  - Can someone help me do it?
  - Will this be beneficial to me?
  - Is this the right time to do it?
- Having a support system of people who believe in you
  Those cheerleaders who are honest and kind and want you to succeed are a great source of motivation
- Finding a role model
  Someone you aspire to be and keeping them in mind when you are doing something
- Doing a WOOP, which is a research-based strategy to help you achieve your goals (Oettingen 2015). This can be very useful

TABLE 4.8 Let's do a WOOP

Wish
Outcome
Obstacle
Plan

for identifying both your goals and the obstacles you will face. WOOP stands for:

- Wish: what do I want?
- Outcome: what will I get?
  Obstacle: what's in the way?
- Plan: what will I do?

For example, it could be that your wish is to go to university. The outcome will be that you will get a degree and have good job prospects; the obstacle could be that you need to have good grades, but at the moment, these aren't too good; and the plan would then be that you will study better and put in more effort to get your wish.

Activity

Think of something you really want to achieve, and go through the WOOP model to help you identify how to get there.

Motivation encompasses resilience, which is the strength to carry on in the face of adversity. Finding that fire that fuels our ideas and gets us going is very important.

▶ MANAGING EMOTIONS

Understanding how you feel and react at a given time and being able to handle those emotions to express them appropriately can help you navigate the world feeling in control. All emotions are valid, necessary and important; experiencing them is part of being human. Some people think that being sad, angry, confused or scared are negative emotions that we must avoid. This is far from the truth, and it is a toxic thought as it negates our feelings and emotions and gives them a bad connotation. It is completely normal to feel all these if you are going through a difficult time, if you have lost a loved one or if someone has been rude to you.

In my previous book (Devis-Rozental 2018), I explored how emotions are our natural way of communicating and how, to our ancestors, emotions were pivotal to their survival. They are our body's way of dealing with external stimuli. All emotions are social because we learn how to express them from our environment and also because when we express them, we impact our social environment too.

Emotions also impact our physical wellbeing. Every time we have an emotion, it instigates the production of hormones, which activates a physical response. For example, if we feel anxious, our cortisol levels will increase, making us feel irritable; our heart rate will rise, and we may begin to sweat. Emotions also influence our motivation, sense of fulfilment and how we make decisions.

Labelling emotions can be difficult as the array of emotions is vast, but being able to express how you are feeling is very important. Words matter because they are our way of assigning meaning to something, and if you can identify how you feel, you will be much better equipped to manage that emotion.

There are many ways to categorise emotions. I find the wheel of emotions developed by Plutchik (2002) quite useful. In this wheel, there are eight basic emotions:

- Joy
- Trust
- Fear
- Surprise
- Sadness
- Anticipation
- Anger
- Disgust

Emotions wheel

Figure 4.4 Adaptation of the wheel of emotions

These emotions are arranged in the wheel in opposites like this:

- Joy and sadness
- Trust and disgust
- Anticipation and surprise
- Fear and anger

I have adapted his wheel of emotions to break it into parts. The first one is looking at the basic emotions and how they are placed against the polar opposite emotion.

According to Plutchik, each of these emotions can become more or less intense and even combine, creating a new emotional state. There are many combinations, but here are some examples:

Joy + trust = love
Trust + fear = submission
Disgust + sadness = remorse
Fear + surprise = awe
Surprise + sadness = disapproval

Intensity of emotions

Each emotion can be experienced with various levels of intensity, which is when it starts to get more complex as there are countless terms to define and express emotions, and these are subtly different. Feeling "worried" isn't the same as feeling "terrified", yet they are both still forms of experiencing fear. Table 4.9 shows how each of the core emotions has subcategories.

I have left some space in each column for you to think of any other terms that might fit.

Plutchik's model is much more complex, and it also includes colours to depict the intensity of the emotion.

Activity

For this activity, think about a time you felt one of the core emotions. Then have a look at Table 4.9 and identify specifically how you felt considering the different terms and reflect on:

• How did you feel?
• What did you think?
• What did you do?

▶ SELF-COMPASSION

I originally labelled this section "self-esteem" in my previous work (Devis-Rozental 2018, 2020). But after further investigating the topic, I felt that esteem wasn't a strong enough word to really identify the notion of unconditionally loving and caring for ourselves, so I have relabelled it self-compassion. Encompassing how we see and value ourselves, self-compassion also integrates how we treat or should treat ourselves. In a world where we have given others online the power to measure our worth based on likes and where some of us only feel loved or worthy if we look or act in a

TABLE 4.9 Some subcategories of emotions

Joy	Trust	Fear	Surprise	Sadness	Disgust	Anger	Anticipation
Happiness	Safety	Worry	Shock	Grief	Hatred	Fury	Vigilance
Pleasure	Hopefulness	Anxiety	Wonder	Regret	Disapproval	Rage	Excitement
Elation	Security	Stress	Awe	Hurt	Revulsion	Irritation	Awareness
Pride	Positiveness	Terror	Shock	Rejection	Repulsion	Bitterness	Patience
Contentment	Supported	Concern	Disbelief	Pensiveness	Dismissiveness	Jealousy	Expectation
Serenity	Acceptance	Apprehension	Distraction	Remorse	Boredom	Annoyance	Interest

certain way, self-compassion allows us to accept ourselves as we are, imperfect and flawed and at the same time inimitable and awesome. According to Neff (2011), self-compassion has three main elements:

- **Self-kindness**
- Being warm and caring towards ourselves
- **Common humanity**
- Knowing that suffering and imperfection are shared human experiences
- **Mindfulness**
- A non-judgemental state where we observe our feelings and thoughts as they are, and we allow them to be. This needs a bit of practice to master

I have identified in Figure 4.5 some ways in which you can become more self-compassionate, and I will go through each of these.

Figure 4.5 Ways to increase our self-compassion

Self-kindness

Being kind to ourselves can be hard sometimes. Being overly critical or seeking perfection can hinder our ability to be kind towards ourselves. Accepting ourselves, how we are with our strengths and limitations, is the first step to self-kindness.

Perfection is overrated

Perfectionism is the unrealistic need to seek perfection or appear perfect. It is also about having very high expectations of others and ourselves. It is a personality trait that can become toxic and lead to mental health issues such as anxiety, depression and lack of self-esteem; it can also hinder our relationships with others.

I must admit that I am a recovering perfectionist. I spent years trying to be perfect in every way, and it was exhausting and unfulfilling, as nothing was ever good enough. This impacted my mental and physical health, and it took me years to acknowledge it and even more to do something about it. In some communities, being perfect is highly regarded at any cost. People spend thousands of money trying to mould themselves into "the perfect human", which, of course, doesn't exist. Society's standards, tainted by filters and unrealistic idealistic ways of life, which are portrayed in social media, television and magazines, put a great strain on our sense of self-worth and our wellbeing.

This is not to say that seeking improvement and self-development is not important. Of course, it is; we should always strive to do our best. The point is to also understand that we are flawed and that that is okay. Perfection is an unattainable goal as it is something we will never be. But knowing this should feel like a huge weight has been lifted. It means we can be who we are with all our quirks and imperfections. It means that we acknowledge them and embrace them. It means that we can forgive ourselves and try again if we make mistakes.

How can we overcome perfectionism?

Be honest and learn to recognise perfectionism in yourself. Can you see yourself in any of these statements?

- Setting unrealistically high expectations of yourself and/or others
- Being overly critical of yourself and/or others
- Procrastinating due to a fear of failing or not doing something perfectly
- Looking for validation from others
- Seeing mistakes as failures
- Avoiding things that may cause you to fail or avoiding new experiences for fear of failing
- Spending a lot of time and energy hiding your flaws
- Feeling extremely vulnerable to others' opinions
- Feeling that your self-worth depends on your achievements
- Being overly cautious and thorough (spending too much time on a task that doesn't require it)
- Worrying over small details
- Continuously feeling like a failure or not good/pretty/skinny/happy/etc. enough
- If you see yourself in some of these statements, you may be a perfectionist.

Look at the bigger picture

Looking beyond ourselves when dealing with difficult or new situations can be useful. Sometimes life can be hard, and you may have to deal with situations that can be difficult in many ways. Learning how to manage your emotions and navigate through those difficult or unfamiliar situations instead of running from them can positively impact your confidence, resilience and sense of self.

Activity

Table 4.10 includes a series of reflective activities that you can do to help you see the bigger picture when you are finding things difficult, feel anxious or worried.

TABLE 4.10 Activities to develop perspective

Activity	Reflection
Time to heal	Even though it may feel like it, is this the worst thing that has ever happened to me? If it is ✓ Take some time to cry or to really feel those powerful emotions whilst checking in with yourself to make sure you are safe ✓ Seek support if you need it; we all need help sometimes, and that's okay ✓ It may take a while, but when you feel able to do so, try putting into practice some of the positive strategies I have shared with you ✓ Eventually, you may be able to see opportunities for growth in the situation and to find the collateral beauty to make this a life lesson that will eventually make you stronger. It is hard, but so worth it! If it isn't ✓ Give yourself the time to feel sad or angry, as it is important to let your emotions out, but do it with the knowledge that worse things have happened to you and you have survived them. Through it all, continue practicing my positive strategies
The staircase	For this reflection, imagine a staircase with ten steps and place your problem where you think it could be ✓ The first step means nothing to worry about, and every step between becomes a bigger problem until you get to the tenth step which means this is the most horrible thing that has ever happened to you ✓ This exercise helps to put things into perspective with some logic
Managing emotion	Ask yourself "Am I behaving in a way that matches the situation?" ✓ This one helps manage your emotions by getting you to think about how you are feeling, by checking in with your body and by helping you bring mindfulness to that very moment ✓ This can be useful to help calm yourself down
Let it go	Ask yourself "Can I control this situation?" ✓ This one helps you identify the things you can control

Activity	Reflection
	Ask yourself "Can I change, adapt or improve the things I can control to make the situation better?" ✓ If yes, do it. ✓ If not, let it go (I know sometimes this can be really hard) ✓ This one will help you feel in control of the situation (remember the circles of control, influence and concern I discussed in Chapter 2)
Worst-case scenario	Ask yourself "What's the worst thing that can happen?" ✓ This one can help you when you are dealing with difficult decisions Ask yourself "If I do this, what would be the worst thing that could happen?"
Best-case scenario	Ask yourself "What would be the best thing that could happen?" ✓ This one brings clarity to a situation and sometimes can give you the courage to take risks
The timeline perspective	Ask yourself "Will this matter tomorrow/next week/next year?" ✓ This one helps you prioritise the things that really matter
Narrative loop	Ask yourself "Am I ruminating and overthinking a situation?" ✓ If you are, what can you do stop the loop and change the narrative? ✓ Remember, you are the author of your story; how it goes is up to you
A positive outlook	Ask yourself "What are the options for me to deal with this in a positive way?" ✓ Think of all the possible positive scenarios for how to manage the situation
A little help goes a long way	Ask yourself "Can someone help me make this better?" ✓ This is a very important question, especially when emotions are high and things could get worse ✓ Asking for help is not a weakness; as I've said previously, we are social beings, wired to connect, and asking others to help us brings them closer to us If you are embarrassed or anxious about asking for help, ask yourself this: ✓ Would I be upset if someone asked me for help on this? ✓ Would I be annoyed if someone asked me for help on this? The answer to these questions is likely no. So, it is worth remembering that it is also very likely that this is the case for someone else, so ask for help if you need it; what's the worst that can happen?

TABLE 4.11 Learning from your mistakes

Mistake	My learning

Seeing mistakes as learning opportunities

Making mistakes isn't fun; it can be embarrassing or sometimes even painful. However, mistakes can be opportunities for learning and developing skills or chances to try something new. Here are some other reasons why making mistakes is important:

- Mistakes can teach you responsibility
- Mistakes can help you to learn to forgive yourself and others
- Mistakes help you learn new things about yourself
- Mistakes can help you make better choices
- Mistakes can improve resilience
- Mistakes can help you become more self-compassionate
- Mistakes are opportunities for growth

So next time you make a mistake, see it as the perfect opportunity to grow. In the table below, you can reflect on past mistakes and think about what you learned from them. This will help you move forward with more self-awareness.

Compromising

Being more flexible with your standards and more realistic with your goals can help you be less strict with yourself and others. Lowering the pressure you put on yourself to be perfect by learning to be happy when you do your best, as this is good enough, is key.

Learn to receive criticism and feedback with an open mind

What others think about you is their problem, and you should try not to worry about it. What you think about yourself is the most important thing. Constructive criticism, being focused on what we do, not who we are, can help us grow and develop. It can also help us learn about ourselves. Hearing others criticise what we do can be difficult and painful, and it can affect how we express our emotions and manage ourselves. At university, there will be times where you will get feedback, and sometimes that feedback will be negative. Nobody likes to receive negative feedback, and learning to accept it can be hard, but it is necessary. Accepting objective feedback when it is needed to improve on something must be constructive. Constructive criticism is not about criticising who you are, attacking you or making you feel inferior. It is about giving you specific, meaningful and useful feedback which should feed forward on what you can do to improve something. If it is not these things, perhaps it is not constructive criticism.

Here are a few tips on how to learn to accept and embrace criticism:

• Avoid the knee-jerk reaction, so stop, breathe and listen instead of reacting at the first sign of criticism
• Actively listen by being attentive to the feedback, and seek clarification if needed by repeating what you heard; this will help you better understand the feedback
• Avoid overthinking it, and focus on the other person's point of view
• Remember that nobody is perfect, including yourself, and there is always room for improvement
• Look for concrete and realistic solutions
• If at any point, the feedback becomes a personal attack, excuse yourself and leave the environment

Positive self-talk

Self-talk is any subjective monologue we tell ourselves about ourselves based on how we see and value ourselves. Words can be powerful, and the way we speak to and about ourselves can have a powerful impact on how we feel about ourselves. Negative self-talk is, therefore, the demeaning and unkind things we think and say about ourselves. It is like a vicious cycle because the more negative, unkind or hurtful we are towards ourselves, the worse we feel. Examples of negative self-talk are "I am so stupid", "I can never get things right", "I look disgusting", "I hate myself", etc. These can be very harmful and impact our overall wellbeing. It is important to identify when we are using negative self-talk and where it comes from. These are some ideas of where this type of talk may stem from:

- Expecting the worst (catastrophising)
- Seeing things as either black or white (polarising)
- Blaming yourself for everything (personalising)
- Exaggerating mistakes or flaws (magnification)
- Dismissing strengths or qualities (minimisation)
- Guessing what others are thinking (assuming)

Positive thinking often starts with positive self-talk. Self-talk is any inner monologue or dialogue you may have with yourself inside your head. These automatic thoughts can be positive or negative. Some of your self-talk comes from logic and reason. Other self-talk may arise from misconceptions that you create because of a lack of information.

If the thoughts that run through your head are mostly negative, your outlook on life is more likely pessimistic. If your thoughts

Figure 4.6 Illustration of the benefits of positive self-talk (author's own)

are mostly positive, you're likely an optimist – someone who practices positive thinking.

Positive self-talk is then how we speak positively about ourselves. It isn't about being cocky or self-indulgent but about being compassionate and honest about ourselves. Research shows that positive self-talk can:

- Reduce stress (Iwanaga et al. 2004)
- Reduce anxiety (Kendall and Treadwell 2007)
- Improve academic performance (Feeney 2021)
- Improve confidence (Tod et al. 2011)

Activity

Try to complete these examples of positive self-talk:

- I am good at ....
- I can do ....
- I can make .... happen
- I love .... about myself
- I can do a great job when ....
- I have a beautiful ....
- My favourite thing about myself is ....
- I feel good when I ....
- I am happy today because ....

Ways to develop positive self-talk:

1. When you catch yourself saying something unkind, ask yourself:
   - Would I say this to a friend?
   - Would a friend say this to me?
   - What would my friend say about me?
   - What would I say to my friend if I heard them saying this about themselves?
2. Identify your strengths, successes, accomplishments and other positive aspects that you consider important.
3. Refocus your attention on your qualities. So, for example, when you look at yourself in the mirror, instead of looking for the

areas you don't like about yourself, make a conscious effort to pay attention to the parts you do like and name them.

4. Use the power of "yet", so, instead of saying, "I am terrible at this", say "I can't do this yet".

Positive affirmations

Similar to positive self-talk, positive affirmations are statements people repeat to themselves that can help challenge negative thoughts and self-sabotaging (use destructive behaviour/attitude towards yourself). Spending just a few minutes every day saying positive affirmations can help improve our performance, calm our nerves by reducing stress (Critcher and Dunning 2015) and improve academic achievement (Layous et al. 2017). One thing that is important to consider is that affirmations must be genuine and linked to your values and beliefs. There is no point in repeating a sentence that means nothing to you, as you will not be invested.

Here are some positive affirmations I have found useful to me:

- I choose happiness every day (I say this to myself every morning)
- I am love (I use this one when I am dealing with someone who isn't kind or considerate, to give me patience and compassion)
- I am the author of my story; let's make it a good one (I use this one when I am having a difficult day)
- I love myself as I am (When I am feeling a bit down, I use this one)
- I am resilient, strong and capable (I use this one when I am nervous)

Positive affirmations can come from many places. I often find inspiration from quotes in music, and I use them as a pick-me-up or as a way to engage with something.

Activity

Think about what inspires you. It could be a song, a poem, a famous figure; whatever it is, find a quote related to it that makes you feel good, and use it as your positive affirmation for at least two weeks, and be mindful of how you feel.

Here are some prompts to help you get started:

- For when I want to feel happy:
- For when I feel worried:
- For when I want to feel safe:
- For when I feel overwhelmed:
- For when I want to feel strong:
- For when I feel lonely:
- For when I want to feel brave:

Gratitude is good for you

The word gratitude comes from the Latin "gratia", which means grace or gratefulness. According to research, gratitude, which is a feeling of appreciation for what you have or receive, is associated with feeling happier. It can help you feel more positive emotions, improve your health, build resilience, make you more optimistic and strengthen your relationships (Fredrickson 2004; McCullough et al. 2002). For example, a study by McCullough and Emmons (2003) found that focusing on the good things that happen to you can have socio-emotional benefits. Seligman et al. (2005) go as far as to say that gratitude can increase happiness. So being grateful is good for you. Additionally, receiving gratitude can make you feel valued, which, in turn, will motivate you to be more generous (Grant and Gino 2010).

The benefits of gratitude can be felt immediately; for example, when someone appreciates you and tells you, you will feel good. However, if there is no consistency, these will wear off over time. To make a lasting impact on our wellbeing, gratitude must be practiced daily and over time. If you want to practice gratitude to make a positive impact on your wellbeing, here are some ideas:

Find the activity that works for you, and give it a go for a couple of weeks to see how it makes you feel.

TABLE 4.12 Gratitude activities

1. Create a gratitude journal

Writing down every day the things you are grateful for can be quite powerful to get you to focus on the good things happening to you. If you choose to journal, make sure it is something you enjoy so it doesn't become a chore. The point is to make it meaningful to you and your experience.

2. Gratitude rock

The idea here is that you find a rock you find interesting or pretty, and you keep it with you, and every time you touch it or see it, you think of something you are grateful for. It can be anything from the sun shining to seeing your friends, anything at all. It doesn't have to be a rock; it can be any object you feel comfortable carrying with you.

3. Accepting compliments

Accepting a compliment from another person can be difficult sometimes. I always tell my friends who find it hard to take the compliment to put it in their pocket for a rainy day. By this, I mean that when they are having a difficult moment, they can stop and think of that compliment and how it made them feel. It is an easy exercise that only requires you to go back in your memory and think of the moment.

4. Expressing gratitude once a day

I do this exercise every morning when I wake up and every night when I go to bed. Basically, you think of three things you are grateful for and number them in your head. For me, this is a great way to start the day, especially if I am in a lot of pain.

5. Seeking the collateral beauty

As discussed previously in this chapter, looking for the good things in a bad situation can help improve our wellbeing. It may not seem natural at first, but trying to find the good in a bad situation can help you learn about yourself and identify new strengths or talents that you may not have noticed. It may take time and reflection to be able to do this, and it may be that whilst you are going through the bad situation, you won't be able to have the perspective and objectivity to think of the good. However, reflecting after the situation, once emotions have settled, can be powerful. It can help you identify your strengths and your resilience and even surprise you with talents you didn't know you had.

Savouring the moment

According to Bryant and Veroff (2007), savouring is paying attention, appreciating and enhancing the things that make you feel good in your life. When you savour the past, you are reminiscing on a memory; when you are savouring the present, you are totally immersed in whichever activity you are doing and appreciating it. For example, when you enjoy a song and pay attention to the sound, rhythm and lyrics. You can also practice savouring the future by visualizing with anticipation and excitement what you will do.

Benefits of savouring

* Predicts higher levels of happiness and satisfaction in life (Bryant 2003)
* Can increase your self-esteem (Bryant and Veroff 2007)
* Improves the quality of your relationships (Pagania et al. 2015)

Activity

Savouring exercises:

1. Enjoy your achievements and successes. In that moment, don't think about what could have gone better; you can do that later
2. Be in the moment at least once a day, and notice what you see, what you hear, what you smell and how you feel
3. Write down three experiences that have gone well and reflect on why they did
4. Write down any act of kindness that you have done over a seven-day period (Otake et al. 2006)

▶ SOCIAL AWARENESS

Social awareness is how we see and understand the world around us, manage our relationships and respond to different situations. It is how we understand and respond to other people's cues, such as facial expressions or body language. It is also our ability to consider the perspectives of others and apply that understanding to our interactions with them. Being socially aware is something that can be learned and practiced. It is influenced by your culture, your upbringing and the way you see the world. It is also neuro-type dependent, which means that the way we understand and see the world and how to interact with it will be different.

Characteristics of social awareness

- Ability to cooperate
- Understanding and expressing gratitude
- Respecting others and ourselves
- Reading the person/room/organisation
- Recognising strengths and talents in others
- Caring for how others feel
- Empathy and compassion
- Understanding and accepting others how they are

How to develop your social awareness

There are many ways to improve our social awareness, and whichever you practice depends on your preferences and how comfortable you feel. Below, I have provided some ideas.

Improving your communication skills

Building good relationships with others requires us to have effective communication skills and a degree of confidence when we interact with others. Communication can be verbal, non-verbal and written.

Mirivel (2014) developed a model called the art of positive communication to create lasting human connections. To develop his model, Mirivel asked the following questions when thinking about positive communication:

1. What communication behaviours show our best selves? That means your potential, what you are capable of doing. What is it that you do when you are at your very best?

2. What small actions make a difference at work and home to interact more effectively?

3. What communication behaviours have a butterfly effect? What small things can you do that will positively impact others, your community and your environment?

Based on these, he developed six behaviours that can have a positive impact on the way we communicate with others (Centre for Positive Organisations 2021). These are:

1. Greet to create human contact

   Greetings are universal in the sense that everyone in the world uses gestures or words to greet each other. They are culturally shaped, as different cultures greet in different ways. When we greet, we create human contact at that moment, and therefore presenting and being our best selves, with genuineness and honesty, will leave a lasting impression and strengthen that human bond. Although this idea is wonderful, not everyone is privileged enough to be able to be their genuine self, for example people from marginalised groups. They may have to mask who they are for self-preservation due to discrimination. Neurodiverse people or some disabled people may also find difficult to make this first contact in the way society expects. I find that being upfront and honest about my limitations from the beginning puts other people at ease.

2. Ask to discover the unknown

   Be curious about the other person, ask open-ended questions (questions where the answer isn't just one word, such as yes or no). So instead of asking:
   - Did you have a good day?
     Ask:
   - What did you do today?

   When we ask people, we will discover and learn more about others. Just remember to listen to the answer before you ask something else. That way you show you are listening with intent, and you are interested in what the other person has to say.

3. Compliment to affect people's sense of self

   What we say, how we say it and what we do has an impact on others. Complimenting and praising others' behaviours will make them feel good. Think about how you feel when someone pays you a genuine compliment. It is a nice feeling. Praising someone with genuineness and being specific can be powerful in building relationships. Complimenting someone for the sake of it, if you don't really mean it, won't have the same positive effect. Giving someone a compliment will take you no time at all, but the effects will last for the person receiving the compliment. Mirivel (Centre for Positive Organisations 2021) states that "when you compliment people you will affect who they are in the moment and who they will become too".

4. Disclose to deepen relationships

We can strengthen our relationships by sharing how we think and feel authentically. This can be difficult if we are scared or worried about how others will perceive us, but being able to be your authentic self and be honest, genuine and show your vulnerabilities can deepen your connection. Here, ensuring that your values align with your behaviour is important, so make sure you share as much as you feel comfortable. Unfortunately, not every situation provides a safe space for disclosing, so don't feel pressured to prioritise building a relationship over your safety. You can disclose by expressing your gratitude, for example, and telling someone how much you appreciate them.

5. Encourage to give support

Mirivel believes that we can transform any ordinary moment into an extraordinary one by supporting others. What we say and do can be used as a source of inspiration when others need it. Think about those who have inspired you by offering you support and encouragement. What did they do? How did they make you feel? Saying some words of support can change someone's day. Encouragement is a gift that lasts and that can have profound effects on others. So ask yourself:

• How do I build people up?
• How can I be their cheerleader?
• What do they need to feel motivated, and how can I encourage this?

6. Listen to transcend differences

When we listen deeply, we can overcome our differences through how we interact with each other. Listening is about accepting; it involves being open without judgement, with full attention and empathy (Mirivel 2014).

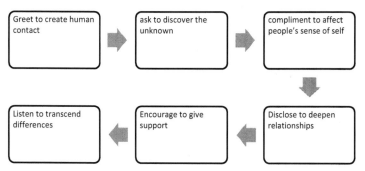

Figure 4.7 Practicing Mirivel's model of positive communication

Activity

For this activity, look at the six steps in Mirivel's model, and think of three things you can do during each step when developing meaningful relationships.

Being aware of those around you

We are all different and communicate in different ways. This is specially the case for neurodiverse people who may find difficult to make eye contact or to shake hands when they greet. This doesn't mean they don't want to interact, so we should be always mindful of that by not assuming it is done with a negative intent. There are two ways in which we can improve our observation skills to have a positive impact on our relationships. The first one is to give our attention to someone when they are talking. That means putting our phones down and acknowledging them. It also means practicing active listening, which involves paying full attention to the person talking to us with all our senses, even if it doesn't look like we are doing it. Traditionally, the main characteristics of active listening have been:

- Pay full attention to the person talking
- Show them that you are listening through your body language
- Avoid interrupting them abruptly
- Respond kindly

However, as we learn more about the brain and how we are all diverse and able to do different things in different ways, I would say that the emphasis should be on every individual finding the way in which they are able to pay attention and participating whilst remaining respectful of others. Some people find it hard to stand still, others to participate. This doesn't mean they are not paying attention.

The second way is to develop a helicopter view to read an environment or a situation. By that, I mean scanning the space and getting a feeling for what is happening to act accordingly. This can be useful in situations where you think you are not going to feel comfortable.

Socialising

Making friends and socialising are important parts of university life. It is a new opportunity to develop meaningful connections and build amazing memories. If you are a sociable extrovert that loves meeting people and get your energy from being around others, you will probably find making friends at university easier. However, this can sometimes be hard for some people, for example, those who are more introverted or those with social anxiety. With the notion that we are each other's environments, here are some things you can do to make others feel included.

- Smile and say "hi" (remember: emotions are contagious)
- Be proactive in getting to know others, but be aware of other people's space
- Offer the seat next to you
- Show kindness and respect
- Give more quiet members of your class space to talk and share their experiences
- Be aware of who isn't engaging, and try to include them
- Ask them, genuinely, how they are doing
- Ask them to sit with you if they arrive alone

We are all different, and some people prefer to be alone, and that's okay, but there is a big difference between spending time alone and feeling lonely. Isolation can negatively affect your mental health, so talk to someone about it if you feel alone.

Setting boundaries

Boundaries are limits, guidelines or rules that you create to feel safe. Setting healthy physical and emotional boundaries is key to protecting your wellbeing; it helps you become more confident, avoid burnout and develop your independence. Which boundaries you set is up to you, and to set them, you must consider what works best for you.

Sometimes people allow others to break their boundaries, or they don't set boundaries at all because they fear being rejected or confronted. This could be due to a lack of self-compassion or little self-awareness. This is why it is important to know what you need and what you want. If you are clear about these things, it will be easier to convey the message to others. Respecting yourself and your needs should never be a reason to feel fear of rejection or confrontation. If others don't respect your boundaries, you may have to question if they are the people you want around you. It may be that they don't understand your needs or are not aware of them, and if that is the case, communication is important to make sure they do. If they do know your boundaries but don't respect them, then you need to ensure that the relationship is not toxic or one that has a negative impact on your wellbeing.

It could also be that setting boundaries is difficult because you feel guilty. If that is the case, here is a list of things that people say make them feel guilty but shouldn't.

- Asking for help
- Taking a break when you need it
- Saying no
- Staying away from toxic relationships
- Standing up for your values
- Making changes to protect yourself
- Feeling emotional
- Challenging inappropriate behaviour
- Asking for what you need
- Being your authentic self
- Practicing self-care
- Asking for adjustments due to your needs (emotional, physical or anything in between)

Tips for setting healthy boundaries

You can set personal boundaries by following the LIMIT model in Figure 4.8:

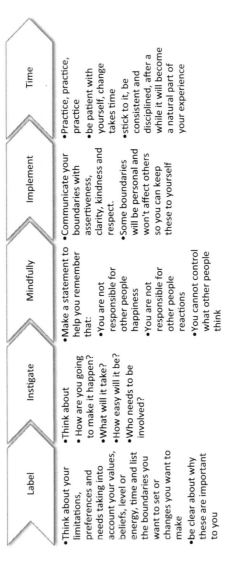

Label	Instigate	Mindfully	Implement	Time
•Think about your limitations, preferences and needs taking into account your values, beliefs, level or energy, time and list the boundaries you want to set or changes you want to make •be clear about why these are important to you	•Think about • How are you going to make it happen? •What will it take? •How easy will it be? •Who needs to be involved?	•Make a statement to help you remember that: •You are not responsible for other people happiness •You are not responsible for other people reactions •You cannot control what other people think	•Communicate your boundaries with assertiveness, clarity, kindness and respect. •Some boundaries will be personal and won't affect others so you can keep these to yourself	•Practice, practice, practice •be patient with yourself, change takes time •stick to it, be consistent and disciplined, after a while it will become a natural part of your experience

Figure 4.8 LIMIT model for setting healthy boundaries

Examples of boundaries you can set:

TABLE 4.13 Type of boundaries

Personal	Social
• Social media consumption • Bedtime routine • Time off to practice self-care • Sticking to your plans • How long you are able to do something • How much you should spend • Where you go • How you identify	• How often you see people • How often you go out • Personal space • When you are able to meet someone • How others should address you • When you choose to allow someone to touch you

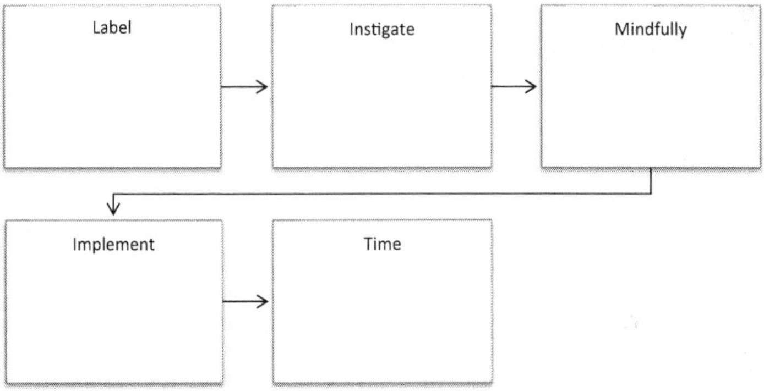

Figure 4.9 Your LIMIT model

When you are ready, follow the LIMIT model and identify the
boundaries that are important to you.

Just as you should set boundaries, other people have their own
boundaries that you must respect. These will depend on
their own lived experiences, and you should always respect
them. If unsure, ask them.

▶ EMPATHY

Empathy is our ability to understand how other people feel from
their point of view, putting ourselves in their shoes and seeing

things from their perspective. It differs from sympathy in that sympathy is feeling bad for someone, while empathy is feeling with that person.

There are two types of empathy; the first type is affective empathy which refers to what we feel in response to other people's feelings – for example, feeling sad when others do too. The second type is cognitive empathy which refers to being able to identify other people's emotions. Not everyone can empathise with others in the same way, and how we do is different depending on who we are, how we think and our experiences, and these differences should always be respected.

Empathy is a complex skill, but it can be strengthened with practice by giving it and receiving it; practicing it can reshape our brain by creating new neuropaths like many of the ideas and activities we have covered in this book.

According to Brené Brown (RSA 2020), empathy has four attributes. These are:

- Perspective-taking, which is being able to see the world as others see it. This may require us to put our own opinions and ideas to one side to be able to fully understand them.
- Recognising emotions in others, which is key to being able to fully understand them. We covered this area previously in this chapter.
- Acknowledging these emotions (labelling them). We have also covered this previously in this chapter.
- No judgement, which means to accept and embrace people for who they are

As we discussed recognising and acknowledging emotions already in this chapter, I will now explore perspective-taking and no judgement.

Perspective-taking

Perspective-taking is the ability to see situations from someone else's point of view. It has three specific areas:

TABLE 4.14 Behaviours that foster empathy

• Kindness

Being friendly, considerate, generous and supportive towards someone.

• Curiosity

Being interested in someone and wanting to know more.

• Respect

Caring and being considerate to other people's feelings, rights and wishes.

• Challenging our biases

Constantly learning and growing in our understanding of inclusivity.

• Becoming more objective

Not taking things personally and being able to see others as individuals and not expect them to behave as we would like.

• Recognise differences, which is being able to acknowledge that we are all different
• Understand influences, which is being able to see why people behave the way they do based on their lived experience
• Look for commonalities, which is to find common ground to strengthen a relationship
• Recognise emotion in others, which is being able to identify how others are feelings based on our own understanding of emotions
• Acknowledge these emotions (labelling them), which is being able to state the emotion and acknowledge it for what it is

Prosocial behaviours to foster empathy

Activity

Thinking about the behaviours that foster empathy presented in Table 4.14, reflect on how you will integrate them as you start making friends at university. Try to be aware of each of these and how you demonstrate them.

TABLE 4.15 Fostering empathy

• Kindness Being friendly, considerate, generous and supportive towards someone.	• I will demonstrate kindness by
• Curiosity Being interested in someone and wanting to know more.	• I will be curious by
• Respect Caring and being considerate to other people's feelings, rights and wishes.	• I will show respect by
• Challenging our biases Constantly learning and growing in our understanding of inclusivity.	• I will challenge my biases by
• Becoming more objective Not taking things personally and being able to see others as individuals and not expect them to behave as we would like.	• I will become more objective by

Conversely, there are anti-social behaviours that hinder empathy and can be damaging to someone in various ways. Here are some of these unacceptable behaviours:

TABLE 4.16 Anti-social behaviours

• Discrimination

Treating someone unfairly for being themselves.

• Negative stereotyping

As previously mentioned, stereotypes are negative generalisations we may make about others. These are typically inflexible and resistant to new information. They can lead to prejudice, even if unintended.

• Bullying and harassment

The repeated and intentional hurting of a person or a group by another person or group, which is offensive and makes someone feel intimidated, degraded or humiliated. This is especially the case if there is an imbalance of power (Anti-Bullying alliance 2022). The bullying can be physical, emotional, written, verbal, in person or online.

• Victimisation

Treating someone badly for standing up for their rights, values, beliefs or those of others.

For a full exploration of equity, diversity and inclusion, check out Chapter 6.

No judgement

No judgement means accepting others for who they are without biases or preconceived ideas. Everything we experience is filtered, categorised and dealt with in a specific way based on our past experiences, environment, culture, etc. Because of these, being able to accept someone with unconditional positive regard, a term developed by Carl Rogers, which means to accept people without judgement, may be hard. However, there are things that we can do to foster an open mind and, therefore, the prosocial behaviours that will help us develop better relationships with others. One way to do this is by learning about the developmental model of intercultural sensitivity which I explore in Chapter 6.

▶ A NOTE ON NEURODIVERSITY

I think it is important to reiterate here that being neurotypical or neurodivergent doesn't mean you can or can't be empathic. It means we all have different ways to show it. As I previously discussed in this book, neurodiversity is about the multiple ways in which we exist, which are all valid. It is important to keep that in mind when reading this book and doing the activities I have included. You will not feel, think or act the same as other people, and that's okay. Knowing this can help you gain perspective as you practice putting yourself in someone else's shoes. It can also help you avoid having expectations from others to be or behave like you. We all love and care for others in our own way, and that's okay. This is not to say that people can be rude or disrespectful; kindness and acceptance must always exist in the way we see ourselves and those around us.

▶ OVERVIEW

Within this chapter, I explored socio-emotional wellbeing within the context of socio-emotional intelligence. There are many ideas and activities within this chapter, some of which may not be useful to you, and that's fine. The key is to find those activities that work for you and to practice them daily to improve your socio-emotional wellbeing. Remember, we are all different, and how we learn and develop depends on many things, so when you find an activity that works for you, great! Keep doing it. However, if an activity doesn't appeal to you, don't worry; try something different. The point of this book is to make it work for you.

The main areas I have covered in this chapter are:

- Developing an understanding of socio-emotional wellbeing so you can improve your confidence and sense of self
- Defining socio-emotional intelligence and its main areas
- Completing a socio-emotional intelligence questionnaire to help you gauge which areas are your strengths and which you need to continue developing
- Exploring self-awareness to help you develop a better understanding of yourself
- Exploring motivation and how to improve it to enhance your wellbeing
- Exploring emotions and how to manage them better
- Exploring the importance of self-compassion
- Exploring empathy and its benefits
- Exploring social awareness and how to improve it

I hope you have found this chapter interesting and useful to continue developing your socio-emotional wellbeing.

▶ REFERENCES

Anti-Bullying Alliance. (2022). *Our definition of bullying*. Available from: https://anti-bullyingalliance.org.uk/tools-information/all-about-bullying/understanding bullying/definition [Accessed 31 March 2022].

Bennett, M. (2013). *Basic concepts of intercultural communication: Paradigms, principles, & practices*. Boston: Intercultural Press.

Bericat, E. (2014). The socioemotional well-being index (SEWBI): Theoretical framework and empirical operationalization. *Social Indicators Research*, 119(2), 599–626.

Berger, C., Alcalay, L., Torretti, A., and Milicic, N. (2011). Socio-emotional well-being and academic achievement: Evidence from a multilevel approach. *Psicologia: Reflexão e Crítica*, 24(2), 344–351.

Bryant, F. B. (2003). Savoring Beliefs Inventory (SBI): A scale for measuring beliefs about savouring. *Journal of Mental Health*, 12, 175–196.

Bryant, F. B. and Veroff, J. (2007). *Savoring: A new model of positive experience*. New Jersey: Erlbaum Associates.

Centre for Positive Organisations. (2021). *The art of positive communication: Six practices to create connection and lead effectively*. YouTube. Available from: www.youtube.com/watch?v=VG0UXBXgB3o [Accessed 21 March 2022].

Critcher, C. R. and Dunning, D. (2015). Self-Affirmations provide a broader perspective on self-threat. *Personality and Social Psychology Bulletin*, 41(1), 3–18.

Devis-Rozental, C. (2018). *Developing socio-emotional intelligence in higher education scholars*. Cham: Springer.

Devis-Rozental, C. (2020). Socio-emotional intelligence: A humanising approach to enhance wellbeing in higher education. In: C. Devis-Rozental and S. Clarke (Eds.), *Humanising higher education: A positive approach to wellbeing*. Cham: Palgrave Macmillan, 15–34.

Emmons, R. A., and McCullough, M. E. (2003). Counting blessings versus burdens: An experimental investigation of gratitude and subjective well-being in daily life. *Journal of Personality and Social Psychology*, 84(2), 377–389.

Eurich, T. (2018). *What self-awareness really is (and how cultivate it)*. Available from: https://hbr.org/2018/01/what-self-awareness-really-is-and-how-to-cultivate-it [Accessed 13 January 2021].

Feeney, D. M. (2021). Positive self-talk: An emerging learning strategy for students with learning disabilities. *Intervention in School and Clinic*, 57(3), 189–193.

Fredrickson, B. L. (2004). Gratitude, like other positive emotions, broadens and builds. In: R. A. Emmons and M. E. McCullough (Eds.), *The psychology of gratitude*. Oxford: Oxford University Press, 145–166.

Grant, A. M. and Gino, F. (2010). A little thanks goes a long way: Explaining why gratitude expressions motivate prosocial behavior. *Journal of Personality and Social Psychology*, 98(6), 946–955.

Iwanaga, M., Yokoyama, H., and Seiwa, H. (2004). Coping availability and stress reduction for optimistic and pessimistic individuals. *Personality and Individual Differences*, 36(1), 11–22.

Kendall, P. C. and Treadwell, K. R. (2007). The role of self-statements as a mediator in treatment for youth with anxiety disorders. *Journal of Consulting and Clinical Psychology*, 75(3), 380–389.

Layous, K., Davis, E. M., Garcia, J., Purdie-Vaughns, V., Cook, J. E. and Cohen, G. L. (2017). Feeling left out, but affirmed: Protecting against the negative effects of low belonging in college. *Journal of Experimental Social Psychology*, 69, 227–231.

Luft, J. and Ingham, H. (1961). The Johari window. *Human relations training news*, 5(1), 6–7.

McCullough, M. E., Emmons, R. A., and Tsang, J. (2002). The grateful disposition: A conceptual and empirical topography. *Journal of Personality and Social Psychology*, 82, 112–127.

Mental Health Literacy. (2022). *Using the right words*. Available from: https://mentalhealthliteracy.org/product/using-the-right-words/ [Accessed 10 October 2022].

Mind. (2020). *Self-harm*. Available from: www.mind.org.uk/information-support/types-of-mental-health-problems/self-harm/about-self-harm/ [Accessed 11 May 2021].

Mirivel, J. C. (2014). *The art of positive communication: Theory and practice*. Oxford: Peter Lang.

van Mulukom, V. (2022). *Psychology of intuition*. Available from: https://valerievanmulukom.com/psychology-of-intuition/ [Accessed 17 February 2022].

Neff, K. D. (2011). *Self-compassion: The proven power of being kind to yourself*. New York: William Morrow.

Oettingen, G. (2015). *Rethinking positive thinking: Inside the new science of motivations*. New York: Penguin.

Otake, K., Shimai, S., Tanaka-Matsumi, J., Otsui, K., and Fredrickson, B. L. (2006). Happy people become happier through kindness: A counting kindness intervention. *Journal of Happiness Studies*, 7, 361–375.

Pagania, A. F., Donatob, S., Parisea, M., Iafrateb, R., Bertonib, A., and Schoebic, D. (2015). When good things happen: Explicit capitalization attempts of positive events promote intimate partners' daily well-being. *Family Science*, 6, 19–128.

Plutchik, R. (2002). *Emotions and life: Perspectives from psychology, biology, and evolution*. Washington, DC: American Psychological Association.

RSA. (2020). *Brené brown on empathy*. Available from: www.youtube.com/watch?v=1Evwgu369Jw [Accessed 22 July 2022].

Ryan, R. M. and Deci, E. L. (2000). Intrinsic and extrinsic motivations: Classic definitions and new directions. *Contemporary Educational Psychology*, 25(2000), 54–67.

Seligman, M. E., Steen, T. A., Park, N., and Peterson, C. (2005). Positive psychology progress: Empirical validation of interventions. *American Psychologist Journal*, 60(5), 410–421.

Tod, D., Oliver, E. J., and Hardy, J. (2011). Effects of self talk: A systematic review. *Journal of Sport and Exercise Psychology*, 33(5), 666–687.

WHO. (2014). *Mental health: A state of wellbeing*. Available from: www.who.int/features/factfiles/mental_health/en/ [Accessed 10 October 2022].

5 Intellectual wellbeing

Exercising our mind

▶ INTRODUCTION

In this chapter, I will explore intellectual wellbeing, the dimension of wellbeing that considers mental activities such as memory, problem-solving, learning and reflecting; the types of activities that stimulate your mind. Intellectual wellbeing is important to consider as it can impact every aspect of your life and all the other dimensions of wellbeing, especially during your time as a student. After all, the brain is the control centre of your body and the key to your intelligence. It is the organ that enables you to live in the moment, reflect on your past experiences and imagine your future near and far. The chapter is divided into two parts: the first part looks at how we learn, with a short overview of intelligence which I will explore from different perspectives to give you a better understanding. I will then share a variety of theories related to how people learn and how to make the most of how you learn. Once the background of how you learn is in place, and you understand they type of learner you are, in the second part, I will share with you the academic skills you need to thrive at university and show you practical exercises to get you ready for your studies. Throughout the chapter, I have included activities and ideas to help you practice your new-found skills.

DOI: 10.4324/9781003317548-5

In this chapter, I will cover these topics:

- The importance of learning how to learn
- Various theories of how people learn
- An overview of neurodiversity
- An understanding of memory and modes of thinking
- The importance of positivity for learning and wellbeing
- A variety of academic skills required for university
- Examples of the types of assignments required at university

▶ PART ONE: LEARNING TO LEARN

To know how to make the most of your intellectual capabilities, it is a good idea first to understand what intelligence is and how you learn. The word intelligence comes from the Latin word "intelligere", which literally means to understand (Devis-Rozental 2018). In the past, intelligence was seen as something predetermined and fixed, so basically, people thought we couldn't develop it. Based on this premise, very negative and harmful stereotypes were developed, and even pseudoscience ideologies such as eugenics (improving a race) were influenced by this. In fact, standardised IQ tests claiming to measure someone's intellect are rooted in racism at a time when scientists were trying to prove that people of colour were intellectually inferior to white people (Reddy 2008).

A better understanding of how our brain works has allowed scientists to evidence that intelligence isn't fixed but something that can be developed and is influenced by our environment. Even though traditionally, people looking at intelligence focused on intelligence as a cognitive or developmental ability, more recently, theorists have begun to look at it considering other aspects. One of these is Howard Gardner (2000), who argues that intelligence(s) are neutral potentials that can be activated depending on our environment. He developed the multiple intelligence theory as he noticed that we all have different talents that can be developed at different levels.

Gardner divides intelligence into these capacities:

- Verbal/linguistic: having verbal skills, ability to learn a language, writing skills

- Logical-mathematical: the ability to analyse problems logically, the ability to do maths problems with ease
- Spatial-visual: the ability to understand and manage spaces, big or small
- Musical: the ability to understand music patterns and perform and compose with great skill
- Bodily-kinesthetic: the ability to use the body with great skill
- Interpersonal: the ability to understand others' intentions and work together effectively
- Intrapersonal: the ability to understand yourself and manage your emotions
- Naturalistic: the ability to be more in tune with nature

Gardner argues that we all potentially have these types of intelligence, but to what extent depends on various factors, such as the experiences and opportunities we have had. I find this idea of looking at intelligence quite reassuring and exciting. It doesn't concentrate on cognitive abilities but considers all sorts of talents. At the end of the day, we are all different, and knowing that by honing our talents, we are developing our intelligence is quite motivating. Nevertheless, there are critics who believe that we all have a single general intelligence, but we use it in different ways. Since we are still learning about our brains, it is difficult to know who is right or wrong. Still, learning about this can give us a new perspective.

Activity

Read the list of Gardner's multiple intelligences, and reflect on the following questions:

TABLE 5.1 Reflection on types of intelligence

Based on how well you know yourself, which of these types of intelligences do you identify as having more of?
Why?
What can you do to continue strengthening it?

▶ DEVELOPING OUR INTELLIGENCE

Lucas and Claxton (2010), other theorists that have studied intelligence, see it as something we can learn and develop. To them, intelligence is a variety of things.

Activity

Below is a list of the ingredients that Lucas and Claxton see as important characteristics of intelligence. Think about each of the sections, and write how you think your intelligence relates to each of the areas that Lucas and Claxton identify:

TABLE 5.2 What intelligence is

Intelligence is . . .	How do you think your intelligence demonstrates this?
Composite which means there are a variety of ingredients needed to be intelligent	
Expandable because it can grow	
Practical because we can apply it to different situations	
Intuitive because there are things our brains pick up much quicker than we can notice	
Distributed because we can use it for different things	
Social because we learn from others	
Strategic because of the methodical approaches we might take	
Ethical which allows us to see the bigger picture or what to do for the best	

This way of seeing intelligence is interesting because it shows that being intelligent may take many forms, making it quite inclusive.

▶ THE CHARACTERISTICS OF INTELLIGENCE

Robinson and Aronica (2009) see intelligence and creativity as intimately linked. They say that intelligence can be learned and offer an interesting view of the characteristics of intelligence. To them, intelligence is:

- Diverse: because it comes in many forms
- Dynamic: because it is interactive, influenced by our experiences
- Distinct: because every one of us is intelligent in our own unique way

They go as far as to compare intelligence to a fingerprint: unique to every one of us. To them, there may be hundreds of ways of being intelligent, so it is so important to challenge traditional views. This is particularly important in this very fast-changing world where we need to develop skills quickly to keep up with advances. Our intelligence has developed through time based on these very changes, threats and advances. It doesn't mean that we are more or less intelligent than our ancestors; they discovered fire, after all. It means we use our intelligence in different ways to solve the problems of the present and the future.

This is also an inclusive way of seeing intelligence, as it considers neurodiversity. We are all unique, as is our way of processing information, and all these ways are valid.

Activity

Think about the three D's that Robinson and Aronica identify as the ingredients of intelligence, and explain how intelligence can be each of these with an example:

TABLE 5.3 Robinson and Aronica's characteristics of intelligence

Ingredients of intelligence	Example
Diverse	
Dynamic	
Distinct	

All these different ideas of intelligence present a great opportunity to rethink intelligence and make our language more inclusive when we are talking about it. After all, the way in which we talk about others and ourselves influences our environment. The stories and narratives we tell ourselves can be fateful. By that, I mean that if, for example, we speak about others in a derogatory way, we will eventually start to believe this is okay and also the truth, which can lead to stereotyping and bullying.

▶ METACOGNITION: LEARNING HOW YOU LEARN

Metacognition is the notion of thinking about the way you think. It's about being aware of your own thought processes and planning, checking and reviewing how to improve them or change them to enhance your learning experiences. The great news is that metacognition is something you can learn and practice. It is about consciously monitoring or checking our memory, the way we understand things and how we solve problems, for example.

There are many tools and ideas to help you learn how you learn, and we will explore some in this chapter.

▶ INCLUSIVE LANGUAGE

When we talk to and about people (and ourselves) with respect, dignity, sensitivity and fairness, we foster an inclusive environment.

We are all responsible for this as part of creating a culture where people feel safe. Some common insults that are widely used are rooted in dated ideas around intelligence being fixed. Terms such as "stupid" or "idiot" were once medical terms to describe people with cognitive disabilities who were deemed to have a low IQ and were therefore treated as inferior. When you are referring to yourself or others, remember to be kind, considerate and caring, and avoid using derogatory or ableist terms such as these. Consider the language you use and the origins of the terms; you may find that many words that you use colloquially have harmful histories. If you want to learn more about positive ways of talking to yourself and others, you can find more information in Chapter 4.

▶ NEUROPLASTICITY

For many years, theorists thought the brain was fixed and hard-wired and couldn't change after childhood, as I wrote previously (Devis-Rozental 2018). Recent research shows this is not the case at all; now we know that people's brains can change well into old age (Voss et al. 2017). Brains are considered to be plastic or pliable. To understand how neuroplasticity works, think of your brain as a sat nav showing you lots of roads going to lots of different places. There are also roads going to the same place but in different ways. When your sat nav knows the way you prefer to get somewhere because you use it time and time again, it will show you little dots as if you were following the crumbs; these represent your usual way of thinking, feeling and doing something. The more you do it, the more it reinforces that path, making it easier to use. However, if the road is blocked one day, your sat nav will find another way to get to the same place. This journey will be new at first, but if you get used to it, it will soon become a normal way of travelling, and that's exactly what your brain does when it creates new pathways. The more you think, do or feel something, the more automatic it will become.

If you don't continue to use the old road, the sat nav may not highlight it as your usual path, and in your brain, that means it may weaken. This way of rebuilding, repairing, strengthening or weakening is neuroplasticity. Pretty clever! This is why it is so important to practice things we want our brains to get used to, so they become the norm. This also means that if we repeat bad habits, they will also be reinforced in our brains, so making sure we choose wisely is good for us and our brains too.

▶ HOW DO PEOPLE LEARN?

There are many ways of learning, and how you learn best will depend on your experiences, preferences and environment. It will also depend on whether you are neurodivergent or have another disability that may influence the way you learn. These are the main schools of thought when it comes to learning. Some are dated, but all offer interesting perspectives:

Behaviourism

Behaviourism is learning that happens as a response to a stimuli/intervention. Traditionally used to train animals, behaviourism can be used to learn a variety of tasks. It is used to learn through association, repetition, reward or punishment. Often called the "carrot and stick" method, behaviourism is quite directive. By that, I mean that direct instruction of what to do, at least at the beginning, is quite common.

- Learning through association is when you make a link between two things. So, for example, when you know that when the fire alarm rings, you need to get out of the building.
- Learning through repetition is when you practice something many times until you feel confident doing it, for example, learning an instrument.
- Learning through rewards is when you are given a prize, a great mark, praise or a present for doing something, and you are motivated to do it because you will get the reward. This is called positive reinforcement.
- Learning through punishment is when you avoid doing something because you know that if you do it, you will get in trouble or be punished.

Activity

Reflecting on your learning:

Think of a time you learned something by repeating it many times. It could be anything, how to do the Rubik's cube or play an instrument, whatever comes to your mind. Now try to go through the steps you used to learn this skill. Then reflect on the following:

1. How did learning . . . make me feel?
2. I found learning to . . . easy because. . .
3. I found learning to . . . difficult because. . .
4. I learn this way when I . . .

Social learning

Social learning theory gives great importance to observing, imitating and modelling behaviour learned from others and the environment around us. We are influenced by our culture, families, friends, the people we study with and even our teachers. Learning from others is something we don't always notice, but it's happening all the time. Learning through observation and modelling has the following processes:

- Paying attention to what you want to learn
- Retaining this information to use later
- Being able to reproduce what you have learned
- Being motivated to do what you just learned

Let's look at the stages through an example:

You see your friend rapping a song and notice that when they do it, they tend to move their mouth in a certain way, so you pay attention. You then recall what your friend did and try to reproduce it because you found it really cool.

Constructivism

Constructivism is the learning theory that explains how people learn by constructing knowledge instead of passively taking in information. Basically, it is the idea that we actively build our knowledge based on what we already know or have experienced. Prior knowledge influences what we learn next. In this theory, the idea that learning is an active process is important. It is the idea that we must make meaningful connections between what we already know and what we are learning.

Scaffolding, which is a staggered way of gaining knowledge, is very much linked to constructivism. We are scaffolding learning when we build on something we know and gain a little more knowledge.

Sociocultural learning

One of my favourite theorists, Lev Vygotsky (1978), developed the sociocultural theory, which is similar to the social learning theory. To him, social interactions are fundamental to our understanding of the world and the way we think. We acquire our sociocultural values and beliefs because of those around us. I would argue that what we learn and how we learn it is also influenced by the internet and social media and other external influences.

Vygotsky developed two important terms when talking about learning. The first one is the zone of proximal development (ZPD), which is the space between what we can learn by ourselves and what we can learn with the support of a more knowledgeable other.

The more knowledgeable other (MKO) is someone who knows more than us about a certain subject. In his theory, Vygotsky identified the MKO as an adult, whereas I think anyone can be an MKO, as we learn things from other people all the time regardless of their age.

Ideas such as peer learning have developed based on this theory and are quite successful. I particularly like his theories because they consider culture as key to our learning and the type of learning we do, whereas other theorists don't.

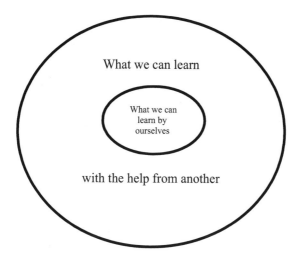

Figure 5.1 Zone of proximal development

Activity

Do you think learning a skill through YouTube is a form of sociocultural learning?

If so, how?

Experiential learning

Learning by doing is another way to explain experiential learning. For example, you may have learned how to bake a cake or paint something. This form of learning is active and requires you to pay attention whilst doing the learning and then reflect on the things you learnt. When you learn by trial and error or by making mistakes, you are learning from that experience. Experiential learning encourages you to take the initiative, make decisions and engage in different ways. Learning through play is a great way to do experiential learning as it allows individuals to engage in something that may be out of their comfort zone and to practice it safely. Simulations, on-the-job learning, travelling and exploring are also examples of experiential learning.

Self-directed learning

Self-directed learning is when you take control of what you learn and how you learn it. During your time at university, this is the most important learning style you will have to develop. Especially in the UK, university courses are designed to give you a lot of time to learn by yourself. This can help you develop independence, self-awareness, self-efficacy and intellectual skills such as analysing, reflecting and evaluating. However, if you come from doing A levels, you may be used to being given information to learn with little time to research any topics in depth or take the initiative on what to do and how to do it. You would have been preparing for exams with set answers, with no space for learning anything outside of specific textbook information. This will not always be the case at university. In fact, more often than not, you will have to make up your mind about how to tackle an assignment and what to put in it. Lectures will often include information to expand your understanding of a topic and may explore things in depth that aren't necessarily linked to your assignment, which can be confusing. Consequently, it is important that you are ready for this type of learning. The fact that you have picked up this book and are wanting to learn about improving your wellbeing shows that you are already practising self-directed learning.

Activity

Table 5.4 includes some prompting questions that you could consider, so you use your time effectively and succeed in your studies. You can make a copy of it and use it for every assignment.

▶ HOW DO YOU LEARN BEST?

There are many tools and techniques around to find out the type of learner you are. On the internet, you will find self-assessment questionnaires that you can do to find out your learning preferences. You may have done some of those and found out that you are a visual (learn by watching), auditory (learn by listening)

TABLE 5.4 Ideas to develop self-directed learning strategies

1. Readiness to learn

How do I learn best for this task?

What are my study habits at the moment?

Is the environment conducive to learning? If it isn't, how can I make it better?

What are my main distractions at the moment, and how can I minimise them?

What is my motivation for completing this task?

How will I be disciplined to complete it on time?

2. Goal setting

Why am I doing this unit?

What is the goal for this unit?

What grade/mark do I want to get?

3. Time management

When is the deadline for this assignment?

How can I plan my time effectively to complete it successfully?

4. Engaging in the learning process

What are my needs as a learner?

How will I engage?

What's in it for me?

Participation is key, so how will I involve myself?

5. Evaluating learning

How can I seek feedback?

How can I apply this knowledge?

Could I explain this to someone?

When do I know I've learned enough?

Do I need support?

Who can give me support for this task?

After I have read the feedback, do I understand it?

What can I do with this feedback?

or kinaesthetic (learn by moving) learner. I think we all learn in these ways depending on our current situation and what we are learning. Research by Hussman and O'Loughlin (2018) found that even when students know their "preferred" learning style and the activities they can use to apply it, students don't use these to learn as they don't work for them. I decided not to include learning styles questionnaires as I think these can be ableist and don't always consider people's culture, language, level of education or neurodiversity.

Instead, here are some recommendations to help you learn better:

- Scaffolding: you should think about what you already know and connect it to what you are learning
- Different media: Use your learning material in different modes (reading, watching a video, talking about it)
- Narrative: we are storytellers and have learned like this for thousands of years, so tell someone about what you are learning
- Spacing: avoid cramming, and instead space out your study so your brain has time to process it

Neurodiversity

In the same way that we all look different, we all learn in different ways. Neurodiversity is the understanding that "people experience and interact with the world around them in many different ways; there is no one "right" way of thinking, learning and behaving" (Baumer and Frueh 2021). It isn't about being more or less intelligent. Within neurodiversity, there are two important concepts, neurotypical and neurodivergent. Individuals considered neurotypical think and process information as expected based on their culture and environment.

Sometimes the way people learn may not be considered the "typical" way, and this can lead to someone being identified as neurodivergent. According to Exceptional Individuals (2022), neurodivergence is "cognitive functioning which is not considered "typical". Neurodivergent individuals may be diagnosed with autism, ADHD (attention deficit hyperactivity disorder), dyslexia, dyspraxia or others. We are all different and unique and learn in different ways. Acknowledging this is important.

Understanding neurodiversity can make us and others feel included and valued. It can also foster inclusive language and a healthy environment. Additionally, finding out how you process information and using this knowledge can help you become a better learner. According to Nat Hawley, the head of community investment at Exceptional Individuals and an expert in neurodivergent thinking, a different way of processing information needs a different approach, so it is worth thinking about how you feel you learn best and developing the strategies that will help you do that.

As you start your university journey, it is also important that you are able to access the support you will need to learn best. Make sure you find out early what support is available in your chosen institution and how to access it. If you have a medical diagnosis, you may qualify for Disabled Students' Allowance, as I mentioned in Chapter 2. Even if you don't consider yourself disabled, it is worth checking if you are eligible for support, and if you need it, ask for it. Don't feel worried, anxious or embarrassed; universities have these services to help you learn, so make sure you use them. It is also important to let your programme leader or the person that manages your programme know that you are neurodivergent so they can put things into place to help you learn and thrive. Some of the things they may be able to do are give you more time during exams or between deadlines, make information available to you before lectures or provide you with different formats to learn. It will depend on your circumstances.

Whether you consider yourself neurodivergent or not, here are some tips that may help you process information better. Remember, we are all different, and some of these may not suit your needs. Additionally, some of the suggestions may not be available to you, but once you start university, you can ask for them based on your needs through a needs assessment.

- Use a colour overlay when you are reading
- Use a ruler to hold under each line
- Take regular breaks
- Use a reading software
- Highlight information
- Be creative about your sources. For example, if you need to read a chapter, also find a summary, a video or a podcast that talks about it to gain a better understanding
- Keep a notebook/online document to write down difficult words
- Use headphones to reduce noise
- Go somewhere quiet to read
- Know when your optimum reading time is
- Be realistic about how much your read (have small goals)
- Change the screen colour to something you feel comfortable with if you are reading on the screen
- Make notes, flow charts, mind maps or storyboards to record as you read

▶ BARRIERS TO LEARNING EFFECTIVELY

To know how to learn, you need to identify what stops you from learning and what barriers you may face. We all have barriers to learning, which depend on our culture, background, opportunities, experiences, abilities and our current situation. Here are some barriers you may face:

Lack of support

Not being supported to learn can have a negative impact on your attitude towards learning new things. I have heard stories from my students who felt they were not supported well by their schools to make informed choices about university, and, due to this lack of support, they didn't apply on time, for example. Unfortunately, education systems are not consistent enough, which can result in inequality of opportunities based on where someone lives or where they come from. In an ideal world, everyone would get what they need to thrive, but this is not the case, and some of us have to work much harder than others to be able to achieve.

Lack of assertiveness

Sometimes people may feel embarrassed to ask for what they need because they don't want to put other people out or are embarrassed. This will only impact their own experience and disadvantage them. However, sometimes the only way to get what you need is to ask for it. If you are someone that feels like this sometimes, remember that this is your learning journey, and it is up to you to seek the things you need. To get started on seeking the support you need, the first thing you need to do is find out what type of support is available at your chosen university. Then you need to know what you need and why. I suggest making a list of what you feel you need and discussing your needs with the appropriate services, as they may have suggestions to support you. If you are worried about forgetting what to say, make a list of the things you want to discuss and refer to it when you ask for support. Assertiveness comes with practice, and it takes time to master so as you develop it; make sure you are kind and compassionate to yourself.

Lack of time

You may be a parent or carer and have little time for studying, or perhaps you struggle with managing your time and tend to procrastinate. Being organised, disciplined and consistent are important skills to ensure you have enough time for everything you need. This is particularly important at university because you will need to manage your own time, something you might not have had to do at school. Suddenly feeling that you have a lot of free time can be overwhelming too, and as a self-directed learner at university, there will be times when you will need to be strict with yourself and use those "free hours" to do your work. I suggest to my students to see university as a full-time job with different tasks and a lot of opportunities for working independently. There are some courses, of course, which are not like this and will have many contact hours (this is what we call the time spent in a lecture, workshop, seminar or tutorial with a lecturer). In the second part of this chapter, I discuss ideas for how to manage your time better.

Lack of self-belief

It may be that you had a hard time at school, a teacher that didn't believe in you or someone who made you feel that you were not intelligent or capable. This can create a barrier as you can develop negative thoughts about yourself or your ability to learn. The good news is that these feelings can be changed with consistency, discipline and practice. Remember, our brain is malleable. Here are some ideas to help you start believing in yourself. I covered this in more depth in Chapter 3.

- Silencing the inner critic; thoughts are not facts
- Positive affirmations; tell yourself nice things as if you were your best friend (which you should be)
- Perfection is overrated, so don't aim for it; instead, aim for growth and development
- It's okay not to be okay; we all have bad days, and that's normal; the important thing is to remember that things don't stay still, and better days will come
- It's okay to make mistakes; this is how we learn

Activity

- Write a list of five things you feel are barriers to keeping you motivated to learn
- Once you have written this list, choose the two that you feel are the harder barriers to overcome
- Now, write an action that you can do to lower this barrier
- Make sure you act on that action and then reflect on the result
- Once you've done it, feel proud of yourself; you've taken steps towards being more empowered and in charge of your learning journey

▶ MEMORY MATTERS

Having a good memory doesn't make us more or less intelligent. However, memory, which is our brain's capacity to store information over time, is an important skill to develop. Our memory has a complex job because we come across new information all the time in different forms, such as images, sounds, smells, meanings, etc. Our understanding of memory is still quite small, but it seems that there are three main jobs that our memory has when it processes information: memory encoding, storage and retrieval.

Many factors influence how long we keep a memory. The way the memory was encoded, how alert and focused we were, how many times we accessed the memory and how important the memory was all play a part in your ability to remember something.

Interestingly, memories are not saved in our minds in a static state, but they change over time based on our experiences and how we talk about them. Every time we retell a memory, we reshape it. This may be why when you are recalling a memory, you always tell it differently.

Memory Encoding	When our brain is faced with new information it needs to categorise it into a way that can be stored easier so that next time we can use this information effectively
Memory Storage	The process of selecting where, when and how much information is stored.
Memory Retrieval	Recalling the information when we need it

Figure 5.2 Memory

Long-term memory

The memories we store over an extended period of time are our long-term memories. The period of time doesn't have to be long; if you remember something that happened hours ago, those count as long-term memories.

Short-term memory

Our short-term memory is our capacity to store a small amount of information and keep it available for retraction for a short period of time. Most of your short-term memories will only be stored for 20–30 seconds unless you rehearse them to be able to keep them.

Strategies for remembering things through multi-sensory learning

Our memory stores information about our experiences considering our senses. Our taste, smell, touch and movement all can help us remember things better because they will go through different paths within our brain and assimilate the information in different ways. This will maximise your opportunities to learn something. Using sensory association by linking the memory to a shape, texture, scent and sound or by using movement can be useful ways to retain information.

Here are some ways to use multi-sensory learning:

- **Act it out**
    Learning by using gestures, movements and props can improve comprehension (Paas and Sweller 2012). This is how small children learn, by using their bodies whilst linking them to an action/animal/situation. You can use this learning to represent, through the gestures, movements or props, how to solve a problem or recall information.
- **Mapping information**
    Creating mind/knowledge maps which are networks that link and group concepts together, finding relationships, meanings

and key concepts helps comprehension. Nesbit and Adelsope (2006) found that students learn better when they "translate" text into a visual representation. You can be as creative as you want with colours and shapes and even use online tools to create these maps of information for learning.

- **Colour**

  Highlighting, contrasting, illustrating or connecting with colours can help you remember things as you retrieve the information by recalling the colour. According to Dzulkifli and Mustafar (2013), colour helps you memorise information by increasing attention, and high levels of contrast between colours has an increased impact on memory retention. For example, using yellow and red or dark blue and white.

- **Association and visualisation**

  Attaching new information to something you already know can help you remember things better. Thinking of a place you know well, like your bedroom, and imagining that you are placing the information in different parts of the room can help you remember them. So, for example, if you need to learn important names, you could use the desk to host one name, the window for another and so on. You can also replace the information for the actual object or place, as this will force you to focus on the mental image. When you need to retrieve the memory, you can visualise the place, and the memory will be attached to it. This type of visualisation can be useful for preparing for exams where you need to retain information and retrieve it fast. Vredeveldt et al. (2011) found that closing your eyes will make visualisation even more effective as you will have less distractions.

- **Self-testing**

  Quizzing yourself on previous material is an effective way to recall knowledge. It can be useful to retain basic facts and more complex ideas, and research suggests that it is better to test yourself repeatedly and develop testing similar to the type of assessment you may have to do (Fiorella and Mayer 2016). For example, if you have an exam coming up, test yourself with the type of questions that you will be asked during the exam.

- **Humour**

  Using things you find funny to link to a memory will make it easier to remember. It could be a picture, a song, a sound or whatever you find funny. Additionally, Tunku et al. (2013) found that recall is enhanced after you watch something funny, even if you are not in a happy mood. So before a test or a presentation, watch something funny that makes you laugh out loud. You may remember it better and feel good as well.

- **Telling a story**

    We are storytellers, and our ability to recall and tell stories is part of our evolutionary history. Research shows that using stories helps organise, retract and predict information (Negrete 2020). So building the memory into a story can be useful for remembering it.

- **Mnemonic acronyms**

    Using keywords to trigger associated memories can be a helpful tool. These words can be created by taking the first letter of each word you are trying to remember and making a new word or sentence with them. One example of this is the acronym SMART (small, measurable, achievable, relevant, timely), used to set goals and objectives. This tactic is particularly useful when learning sequential or repetitive tasks and ideas (Radović and Dietrich 2019).

- **Rhythm and rhymes**

    Very useful for connecting new learning with the knowledge you already have to recall information fast. Rhyming information helps your brain encode it easier. Rubin (1998) found that when a song used two words that rhymed, students were able to remember it better than with no rhyming words.

- **Sleep on it**

    Your brain processes and then stores information whilst you are asleep, and sleep deprivation can actually reduce your ability to learn (Ellenbogen et al. 2006). So instead of spending all night trying to memorise information and therefore not sleeping, spend some time before bedtime reviewing the information and then go to sleep.

- **Talk to yourself**

    Talking to yourself or talking aloud about the material you are trying to memorise or learn can be effective ways to learn them. Research shows that people who explain things to themselves learn them more effectively (Fiorella and Mayer 2016). Part of this learning involves questioning yourself – does this make sense? How does it make sense?

- **Teach it to someone else**

  Being able to recall information by explaining it to another person helps people learn it themselves. According to researchers, learning by teaching is unique because in addition to you having to explain something to a peer, you will need to prepare for doing so as well as interact with your peer, and this helps you to create deeper meaning and therefore having a long-term understanding (Fiorella and Mayer 2016).

- **Chunking**

  In this type of activity, you group individual pieces of information into larger groups. This is useful for remembering a long list of things. Bor (2012) states that our natural tendency to make connections and see patterns is good for our memory, and he defines three sides to chunking: searching for the chunks, memorising them and using them effectively. If you've ever memorised a phone number by grouping individual numbers together, that's chunking.

▶ MODES OF THINKING

Knowledge is important, but what is more important is how you use this knowledge. Thinking critically and creatively are ways to use this knowledge, and as a student, these are key. The American psychologist Joy Paul Guilford (1959, 1967), who believed that intelligence was multidimensional, developed the terms "divergent" and "convergent" thinking to explain how we think differently.

Divergent thinking

Divergent thinking is the thought process you use when you generate a variety of creative solutions or ideas (Robinson 2016). Studies show children have a higher divergence capability than adults. This may be because, as adults, we are faced with very real situations that require us to think logically or because we have been traditionally discouraged from playing, dreaming and creating. Divergent thinking happens when we are able to come up with different ways of doing something, when we encourage different perspectives or when we can express ourselves freely. This makes our environment important to consider if we want to foster divergent thinking.

Ways to foster divergent thinking:

- Mind maps
- Brainstorming
- Debate
- Open-ended questions

Convergent thinking

Convergent thinking is the thought process you use when you think about facts in a logical manner. You may use convergent thinking when you are doing an exam that requires a specific answer. It is the type of learning that is usually encouraged in schools and can be important when, for example, making serious decisions. For example, you use convergent thinking when you evaluate something by looking at the pros and cons. It is about looking for concrete, tangible solutions.

Ways to foster convergent thinking

- Making lists and following them
- Memorising facts
- Checklists
- Following a recipe

Lateral thinking

Lateral thinking is when you use both divergent and convergent ways of thinking at the same time, such as being able to approach a problem from different angles. This is something you probably do every day without even noticing. When you leave your house following directions, you are using your convergent thinking, but when you have to navigate the roads, traffic and any unexpected things, you use your divergent thinking. According to Forbes, lateral thinking is the most valuable skill in times of crisis.

Ways to foster lateral thinking

- Curiosity
- Finding alternative solutions
- Challenging your way of thinking
- Puzzles
- Word games

▶ GROWTH MINDSET

This is the way of acknowledging our minds, talents and ideas as things we can develop.

▶ POSITIVITY FOR WELLBEING

Positivity is the tendency to be optimistic about life, something which, in turn, has a positive impact on our wellbeing. Research shows that positive thinking reduces stress, increases immunity and makes you more resilient.

Developing a positive mindset

A positive mindset is an intellectual and emotional attitude in life that focuses on the good things and expects positive results.

- It's about reframing the bad or negative situations/outcomes
- It can be developed by practicing it every day, as it rewires our brain
- It's great for our wellbeing

The health benefits of positive thinking

Researchers continue to explore the effects of positive thinking and optimism on health. Health benefits that positive thinking may provide include:

- Increased lifespan
- Lower rates of depression
- Lower levels of distress
- Greater resistance to the common cold
- Better psychological and physical wellbeing
- Better cardiovascular health and reduced risk of death from cardiovascular disease
- Better coping skills during hardships and times of stress

It's unclear why people who engage in positive thinking experience these health benefits. Some theorists believe that having a positive outlook enables you to cope better with stressful situations and builds resilience, which reduces the harmful health effects of stress on your body.

Studies have shown that positive and optimistic people tend to live healthier lifestyles – they get more physical activity, follow a healthier diet, and don't smoke or drink alcohol in excess, which may contribute to these health benefits.

Barriers to developing a positive mindset

Even though we may have the predisposition to be optimistic, having a positive mindset doesn't always come naturally, and there are barriers to developing it. Here are some of these:

- We've been conditioned into believing only certain things can bring us happiness, sometimes focusing on material things. However, research shows that focusing on experiences or being kind to others will make us happier.

- We tend to compare ourselves with other people; this is especially prevalent in our society, with social media being a trigger for wanting more, doing more or achieving more as we compare our lives to others, and this is harmful for our self-esteem.
- We get used to things and then want more. Research shows that the more you have, the more you will want. We adapt to things and will want more. Finding the balance and having enough should be the goal.
- Seeking perfection will always be unfulfilling, and that can be a barrier to a positive mindset.

Characteristics of people with a positive mindset

Research shows that people with a positive mindset are at an advantage in many ways. Additionally, researchers have identified some of the distinct characteristics of people with a positive mindset (Cameron 2021). People with a positive mindset:

- Are a source of energy and motivate others (positive energisers), so people will want to spend time with them as they will feel energised afterwards
- Enjoy the unexpected, so take calculated risks
- Cope better with changes and develop their resilience
- Seem friendlier
- Seem more attractive (it is true, research backs this up!)
- Are generous
- Are more successful
- Better manage negative emotions

So, whichever way you look at it, developing a positive mindset is great for us!

Positivity myths

People have misconceptions about what it means to be positive, and this can sometimes be harmful and become toxic positivity. Here is a list of positivity myths and why they are not true:

- "I must be happy all the time": having a positive mindset doesn't mean that we have to always be happy, smiling and cheerful. It is about our outlook on situations and how we approach them.
- "I can't show my negative emotions": all emotions are important, necessary and allowed; what matters is how we react to them. It is okay to be sad, disappointed, angry or annoyed, and expressing these emotions is good for our health. However, using them to be destructive, vengeful or violent isn't okay.
- "I can't spend time feeling sad": feeling sad is an important part of life. Allow yourself to feel what you are feeling; give yourself what Paul McGee (2016), the SUMO Guy, calls "Hippo time", a time to wallow and feel the sadness without letting it overtake your life. Once you've had your Hippo time, let the feelings go and return to your happy place. If these feelings don't subside, make sure you seek help, as it could be that there is something deeper to explore.
- "I must always agree with other people": "no" is not a bad word, but some people think that using it means they are being negative. But "no" can be a powerful word to safeguard your wellbeing. I know it is sometimes difficult to use it, especially if we like pleasing others, but knowing your boundaries is very important as part of being and becoming more positive.
- "I can fake being happy": people can read your real emotions, so don't hide them. Be genuine and true to yourself.
- "We are born positive": this is simply not true; optimism can be learned and developed by changing daily habits. This takes time and effort, but doing it in small steps, with consistency and discipline, will pay off.

Habits and exercises to develop a positive mindset

Here are some exercises to help you develop a more positive mindset:

- Labelling emotions, which is when you understand and name the emotion you are feeling at a given moment. I discuss this in depth in the socio-emotional wellbeing chapter.
- Reframing problems into opportunities, which is when you are able to see a problem as a chance to learn from it. This is also the case for making mistakes. If we make a mistake, we should not punish ourselves but rather see it as an opportunity for growth. At the end of the day, we are all human and make mistakes, and this is part of our trial-and-error way of learning about the world around us. It is important, though, to ensure that whatever you are doing, you are always safe and aren't putting yourself in harmful situations.
- Self-compassion, being kind to yourself and treating yourself as if you were your best friend, because you should be.
- Positive affirmations, which I cover in depth in the socio-emotional wellbeing chapter.
- Positive thinking, which is approaching unpleasantness in a more positive and productive way.
- Savouring the moment and enjoying being where you are. Put your phone down, look up to the sky, smell the flowers or listen to your friends attentively.
- Helping others is great for your wellbeing and triggers happy hormones for them and you: win-win.
- Laughter, believe it or not, can help you develop a positive mindset. Research shows that when we laugh, there are many positive things happening to our bodies and our mood. The picture below shows you what happens when we laugh.

Activity

Reflect on these questions:

1. Do you consider yourself a positive person?
2. How do you know?
3. What can you do to become more positive?
4. What benefits could this have in your life?

Figure 5.3 Illustration of the benefits of laughter (author's own)

▶ PART TWO: ACADEMIC SKILLS REQUIRED AT UNIVERSITY

We've already identified that learning increases your confidence, and getting ready to go to university by identifying and learning the basic skills you need can help you settle and achieve. Although every university is different, as is every course, there are some common things you should be aware of, or at least I wish someone had told me. By now, if you have done the tourist metaphor activity in Chapter 1, you will have reflected on some of these already. If you haven't, I recommend you do it to give you some sense of direction. For a more in-depth look at academic skills development, I would recommend checking out Stella Cottrell's books, which are very comprehensive.

Time management

As we saw earlier, managing your time at university is key to your wellbeing. Here are some useful activities that can help you learn to manage your time effectively:

* Small pockets of time: these are the short periods of time where you may have a window to be productive. It could be anything between 5–30 minutes. You can find them by jotting down everything you do for three to five days. You will be surprised at how many pockets of time you identify. You can use these productively by listening to a podcast, catching up on some reading or even checking your grammar. You can find them by highlighting the times you are waiting for something, or when you have a minute and your go-to is social media. It could also be that early in the morning, before you start your day, you find some time. Of course, this doesn't mean that you must be busy all the time. In fact, you could find the small pockets of time to rest, meditate and relax.
* Understand procrastination: this is a big one. The reasons why we procrastinate may surprise you. When people procrastinate, they are unnecessarily, but not always on purpose, delaying an important task. Some people procrastinate because they find something difficult, boring or unpleasant. Perfectionists also procrastinate because they think they are never going to get something perfect. There is another type of procrastinator who enjoys leaving things to the last minute and the adrenaline rush this gives them. Whichever type of procrastinator you are, regularly putting things off can have a negative impact on your wellbeing. It will increase your levels of stress and anxiety and even your life satisfaction. Being kind to ourselves and understanding why we do it can help us overcome procrastination.
* Time management: be realistic about how long activities take and plan for them. Doing a timetable can be useful for this. Make sure that you add travelling time, resting time and eating time so you also take care of your basic needs.
* Small goals: Setting yourself short goals that will add up to a large one will be less daunting than cramming it all in. I give

myself daily word count goals when I am writing, and this really helps me feel I have achieved whilst contributing to the overall word count.

- Pomodoro Technique: this is a useful technique where you choose a task and set a timer for 25 minutes to work on your task. When the timer stops, you stop and take a five-minute break and then start another 25 minutes. It is really important that every four cycles, you give yourself a longer break (20–30 minutes). This will help you stay on task but also rested and relaxed. Remember to hydrate during the breaks.
- Find your rhythm: every one of us works in a different way and finds some times during the day more productive than others. Keeping an eye on when you feel more energised and work better will help you make the best of your day. For example, I work better in the mornings, so I do my writing then.

Organisational skills

Organisation is key when we want to learn effectively. One great tool to get you planning for your learning is doing a SWOT analysis. This tool, which is normally used in business, can be great to get you thinking about your learning. It is divided into four quadrants and asks you to reflect on them. These are your Strengths, Weaknesses, Opportunities and Threats. The tool can be used to focus your mind on reflecting on your life and the areas that can have an impact, either positive or negative, for optimum learning.

- Strengths
  The positive attributes, talents and skills that you have which are under your control
- Weaknesses
  The areas where you feel less confident about which can have an impact on your learning from a personal point of view
- Opportunities
  The external factors that can help you learn effectively
- Threats
  The external factors that can have a positive impact on your learning

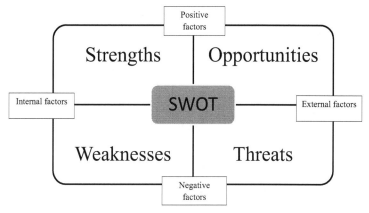

Figure 5.4 SWOT analysis

Some examples of the type of questions you can ask yourself within each of the quadrants to identify key aspects are these:

STRENGTHS

- What am I good at?
- What skills do I have?
- Which are useful for this situation?
- How can I use them?
- What do I know already?
- How can I use this knowledge?
- What achievements am I more proud of?
- Which of my strengths can help me get to where I want?

WEAKNESSES

- What do I need to improve?
- What are my main gaps in learning?
- What do I feel embarrassed about?
- What do I try to do but don't seem to improve?
- What holds me back from doing something?
- Where do I lack experience?

- When do I feel like I don't know something?
- What distracts me from learning?

OPPORTUNITIES

- What support is available to help me improve?
- What new technology can help me learn better?
- What opportunities are around me?
- How do I learn about my optimum working time?
- What do I want to achieve?
- What do I want to learn?
- What should I be prepared for?
- How can I increase my network of support?

THREATS

- What unexpected problems may happen?
- What can set me back from achieving something?
- What external factors can affect my learning?
- What obstacles do I face at the moment to get me to where I want?
- Could any of my weaknesses lead to a threat?
- Is my situation changing and out of my control?
- What are things I have no control over?
- What challenges might impact my intellectual wellbeing?

Here is a blank SWOT for you to complete with your own reflections; you can use the prompts above or your own questions. This is a really useful tool to understand where you are at in your learning and what to do to continue developing it.

Types of tasks you may have to do at university

Whilst at university, you will need to complete a variety of tasks in order to successfully complete a unit. These will vary and

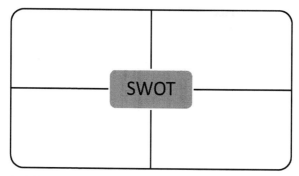

Figure 5.5 Your SWOT analysis

depend on the type of course you are doing, and their names will differ too. Traditionally, arts-based programmes may be more hands-on than other programmes, but, at least in the UK, you will have to complete a series of academic tasks that will be evaluated and give you the marks you need to pass your course. The types of assignments can be grouped into four categories:

- Doing
- Making
- Speaking
- Writing

Within these, there will be a variety of tasks that you may be asked to do. Let's go through some of them.

Doing

Typically practical, hands-on activities to demonstrate knowledge/skills to a predetermined standard.

Types of doing assignments

- Observation
- Role play
- Simulation
- Portfolio activity

- Placement
- Work experience

Making

For these types of assignments, you may need to create something – a concrete thing or a model/design – and, in the process, may use research, exploration and experimentation.

Types of making/creating assignments

- Blog
- Essay plan
- Lesson plan
- Concept map
- Portfolio
- Poster

Speaking

These tasks allow you to address learning outcomes through oral interaction and presentation skills. They can be scary but are very useful to build your confidence and get ready for employment.

Types of speaking tasks

- Debate
- Presentation
- Pitch
- Conference
- Viva
- Interview

Writing

You need to demonstrate knowledge and skills through written tasks. These tasks enable students to express ideas for different purposes and to different audiences through different media.

Types of writing assignments

- Abstract
- Essay
- Report
- Grant application
- Open book exam
- Logbook
- Questionnaire
- Question bank
- Exam
- Reflection
- Annotated bibliography
- Discussion board

Doing-Making-Speaking-Writing

Sometimes you will have to do assignments that mix different forms to demonstrate your knowledge and skills through tasks that draw on two or more of the assessment types.

- Thesis (sometimes called exegesis, dissertation or capstone project)
- Case study
- Field report
- Research project
- Review

Whichever assignment you are given, remember to:

- Meet the learning outcomes set
- Include a reference list (of what you have used to substantiate your assignment)
- Have the format specified
- Meet the word count
- Meet your deadline

Keywords you may find in your assignment briefs

The keywords that signal what you are expected to do in an assignment and are normally included in the learning outcomes within a brief or a unit handbook have probably been taken from Bloom's taxonomy (Anderson and Krathwohl 2001), a framework for categorising how we learn. The taxonomy has five main categories, with subcategories within each of them. Table 5.5 shows the keywords, an explanation and the other words you may come across within an assignment.

When you get an assignment, it is important that you are clear on what you have to do. Therefore, always check your assignment brief and make sure it makes sense. Identify the keywords, such as those above, and ensure you understand them, as these will signal what you will have to do. Once you have done that, you should use a method that works for you to identify your learning

TABLE 5.5 Adaptation of Bloom's taxonomy

Keyword	Subcategory
Create (produce original work)	Design, construct, develop, formulate, instigate, investigate assemble, modify, generate, invent
Evaluate (justify or make a decision)	Argue, defend, support, critique, select, decide, judge, justify choose, relate
Analyse (break into parts and find connections)	Explore, organise, compare, contrast, distinguish, examine, experiment, test, differentiate, question, break down, illustrate, associate, diagram
Apply (use information in a different context)	Implement, solve, demonstrate, interpret, operate, execute, identify calculate, predict, model, perform, present
Understand (comprehend and explain ideas)	Describe, explain, identify, recognise, select, report, paraphrase, restate, summarise, interpret, classify, translate, discuss
Remember (recall information)	Memorise, recall, repeat, define, duplicate, name, list, recite, match, identify, label, recognise

outcomes (highlight, colour, number, map), and as you complete your assignments, use your chosen method to ensure you fully meet each outcome. Below is an example of learning outcomes for an assignment; I have made the keywords **bold** so you get an idea.

- **Explore** the idea of learning within higher education
- **Identify** the main types of learning
- **Evaluate** why these are important

There are some types of assignments which may get confusing if you have never come across them. This may be the case for reports and essays, for example. Table 5.6 illustrates how these are different:

TABLE 5.6 Reports vs essays

Academic Reports	Academic Essays
• Contents page with all the sections • Introduction • Sections divided into headings • You can have tables, charts and graphs • Conclusion • Reference list • Based on practice backed up by theory • Don't include examples of other companies • Writing in academic language • May have less references within text as the focus is on the practice	• Introduction (telling the reader what the essay is about • Main body (making it happen) based on theory by citing relevant sources and linking it to examples • Conclusion (telling the reader what happened) • Do not use headings • Do not use pictures, graphs, etc (unless specified) • Written in the third person (unless specified) • Reference list with all the sources you have used in the essay, making sure the preferred referencing guidance has been used

Other types of activities or assignments that can help you develop your academic skills

1. Essay plans

An essay plan is a useful tool to help you plan your essay. It is important to start it early and to be clear about what you want to include to meet the learning outcomes of an assignment. It normally would include:

- Introduction: tell the reader what the essay is about (in the present or future tense and the third person)
- Main body: separate it in paragraphs including your idea/argument, the link to theory/evidence (referenced) and an example (in the present or past tense, but be consistent)
These paragraphs should be between five to eight lines (longer is difficult to read, and shorter won't be long enough to make your point)
- Conclusion: writing in the past tense, tell the reader what you told them. No new sources, no citations or any new references should be included.
- Reference list: a list of the sources you used on your assignment

Example essay plan about emotions in higher education:

TABLE 5.7 Example of an essay plan

Learning outcomes	Structure	Evidence
In this essay, I will have to show that I: Understand students' emotions in HE Explore its impact on their studies Explain the importance of seeking support in HE	Introduction • This essay explores emotions in students within higher education (HE). In order to do so . . . . Main body • Paragraphs one to four • Explain student emotions in HE (theory, argument, example) • Explain why these are important (argument, theory, example) • Paragraphs five to nine • Introduce the idea that emotions can impact students' studies (theory, argument, theory, example) • Explore how emotions can impact students (theory, theory, argument)	Look at the general theory of emotions and link to higher education Add any important definitions Add a source about the impact of emotions on students Find some contrasting opinions on seeking support and self-efficacy Remember to make sure the learning outcomes have been met and the question or argument has been answered

Learning outcomes	Structure	Evidence
	• Begin linking to the idea of seeking support (argument) • Paragraphs 10–13 • Explain why seeking support is important (theory, argument, example) • Explain how students can seek support (example, argument theory) Conclusion • Conclude by bringing together all the main points • Signal to any new learning and importance of the topic References • Only include the sources you have actually read and used in the essay	Use the referencing system for your university and make sure all the sources are included and properly referenced

2. Reflection

Reflective writing is a type of writing where you go over what you have done and think about it in order to learn something from it. It is about learning and gaining insight from a previous experience. Some of the advantages of reflecting are:

- Improves performance
- Reassess behaviour
- Changes attitudes
- Asserts our way of being

Reflection is not about judging, criticising, belittling, ruminating, blaming or being biased. It is about seeing things with perspective for what they are and learning from them.

In order to be able to reflect, you will need:

- A willingness to do it
- Time to do it
- Open-mindedness

There are various types of assignments that may ask you to reflect. Here are some examples:

- Journal
- Portfolio
- Diary

- Reflective essay
- Blog
- Conversation

When you write a reflection, you link new knowledge gained from experience and from theory, or resources you have read, to your lived experience, taking into account your thoughts, emotions and the situation in which you are reflecting.

There are many models of reflection which can be useful as they give you a framework from which to think about your experience. Here are some examples that you may find useful:

Driscoll (1994) model of reflection:

- What (happened)?
  - Describe
- So what (what does this mean)?
  - Analyse
- Now what (what will you do with this new knowledge)?
  - Evaluate

I really like Driscoll's model as it is easy to follow.

Gibbs (1988) model of reflection

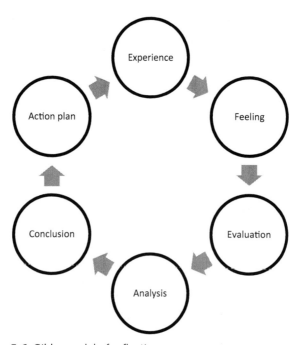

Figure 5.6 Gibbs model of reflection

Gibbs' model is useful if you want to delve into your emotions as part of the reflection; it also breaks things further.

Atkins and Murphy (1994) cycle of reflection

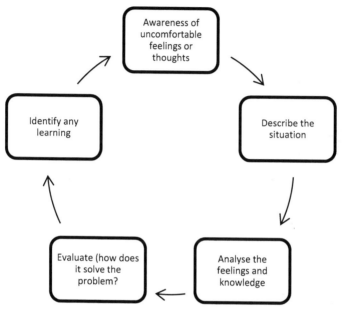

Figure 5.7 Atkins and Murphy cycle of reflection

This model is easy to follow and useful as it gives clear prompts.

Whichever model you decide to use, here are some prompts to remind you what to do and to ask you to reflect on how to do it:

TABLE 5.8 Prompts for reflection

Be	personal but not biased	How can I do this?
Be	insightful but not judgemental	How can I do this?
Be	focused but balanced	How can I do this?
Remain	formal and academic	How can I do this?
Link	theory to your own experiences	How can I do this?

3. Annotated bibliographies

This type of activity requires you to identify a series of relevant texts on a defined topic, and following a referencing style (your university will advise on which you should use), write the reference. You should then summarise and evaluate what you have read. This is a useful activity to understand the texts you are using.

4. Mind maps

These are useful visual representations which use lines to divide, link, organise or group information (Scott 2021). This type of diagram can be used to identify and organise information. It should have tiers and clearly demonstrate the relationships/branches between different areas.

5. Note-taking

Being able to listen, pay attention, understand and jot down ideas during a lecture can be quite complex, especially if you haven't practiced doing it. Here are some tips that you may find helpful for taking useful notes:

Notes from reading

- Scan the text to identify themes, keywords and overall meaning
- Highlight keywords
- Avoid copying too much text; instead, try to paraphrase
- Make immediate note of the source you are using to reference it later
- Focus on the task you are reading for, and avoid going on a tangent. If the information is interesting but not relevant, put it aside to read later.
- Use visual representations of ideas to help you remember something
- Remember that if you are set some reading, they probably don't mean a whole book but a section of the book or an article from a journal. Reading a whole book will not be necessary unless specified.

Notes during a lecture

- Develop your own personal shorthand/language by using memorable things that work for you

- Use visual representations of ideas by adding arrows, circles, bubbles, etc
- Avoid taking notes on information you already know
- Listen for keywords and phrases
- Use coloured pens if that works for you
- Check your notes soon after your lectures so they make sense to you

Tips for completing assignments successfully

- Organise your work
- Create a master document where you include all the sources you have ever used. Make sure these are up to date and that you have used the required referencing method.
- Always include a reference list at the end of your work
- Keep notes from different units separate so you can find them easier
- Keep a timetable with deadlines so you know when you need to hand in your assignments
- Ensure you start your assignments early
- Seek support if you don't understand something

When you are writing academically, you must:

- Form arguments based on theories and ideas written in academic sources
- Substantiate (use theory to back up your ideas)
- Paraphrase (write what you have read in your own words)
- Think critically (explore the information, and avoid accepting it without checking if it is real, if it makes sense and if it can be supported by theory)

1. Aim for clarity
   - Use simple sentences
   - Short sentences
   - Using language you understand
   - Paragraphs should be five to eight lines maximum
   - Use connectives to link paragraphs
   - Always keep in mind the subject

2. Be impersonal, unless you are asked to reflect and use the first person
   - Avoid personal pronouns such as I/we/you. Instead, use phrases such as:
     - It can be seen that . . .
     - There have been a number of . . .
     - It has been discovered/found that . . .
     - It could be suggested that . . .
     - On reflection, it could be said . . .
3. Be objective
   - Avoid personal/subjective words such as "nice", "usual", "wonderful"
   - Avoid questions
   - Avoid apologies – "I am afraid that . . ."
4. Avoid weak arguments
   - Emotive language ("poor children", "the needy mother", "I like this idea")
   - Attacking a person
   - Unsubstantiated opinions ("I think", "I hope", "I want")
   - Misrepresentations
   - Ignoring opposing reasons
   - Suggestive language ("obviously", "naturally", "of course")
   - Generalisations
5. Check your academic writing skills
   - Avoid contractions ("can't", "won't", etc)
   - Proofread your work
   - Spell-check everything
   - Be concise by cutting unnecessary words
   - Be specific and precise

Referencing your work

One of the important aspects of university is academic integrity. As part of this, you will need to learn to reference and cite the material you use. If you don't, you may commit an academic offense. Learning how to reference and cite takes time and effort. Each university and each field may have its own referencing system. Some use Harvard, Chicago, APA or other types.

Referencing is when you write the source at the end of a paper, whilst citing is when you use the source within your text whilst acknowledging it. You can see citations within the text in all of my chapters and a reference list at the end of each chapter.

You should find out which referencing system is used in your chosen university and familiarise yourself with it. Seek support from the library or study skills centre if there is one to help you learn how to use it. This may seem like a boring activity, but it is necessary and will save you time and effort in the long term. I recommend you create a master document where you put all the sources you have read, referenced in the preferred style, so you can go back to them any time you need them. I wish someone had given me this advice when I was doing my undergraduate degree, as it would have helped me greatly. Also, make sure you reference everything you read as you find it so it is easier for you later.

▶ OVERVIEW

Throughout this chapter, I have explored a lot of different ideas related to your intellectual wellbeing. I hope you have found them useful and learned something you can use as you move onto your next stage, whatever it may be. This chapter was divided into two parts: the first one looked at how you learn, and the second one looked at academic skills development. Here is an overview of what I have covered in this chapter:

- The importance of learning how to learn to develop self-awareness of how you learn best
- Various theories of learning so you can identify when you use them and how
- An overview of neurodiversity so you have an understanding
- An understanding of memory and modes of thinking to help you develop them further
- The importance of positivity for learning and wellbeing
- A variety of the academic skills required for university so you feel ready for studies
- Examples of the types of assignments required at university with opportunities for you to practice some

▶ REFERENCES

Anderson, L. W. and Krathwohl, D. R. (Eds.). (2001). *A taxonomy for learning, teaching and assessing: A revision of bloom's taxonomy of educational outcomes: Complete edition.* New York: Longman.

Atkins, S. and Murphy, K. (1994). Reflection: A review of the literature. *Journal of Advanced Nursing,* 18, 1188–1192.

Baumer, N. and Frueh, J. (2021). *What is neurodiversity?* Available from: www.health.harvard.edu/blog/what-is-neurodiversity-2021112326 45#:~:text=Neurodiversity%20describes%20the%20idea%20that, are%20not%20viewed%20as%20deficits [Accessed 22 July 2022].

Bor, D. (2012). *The ravenous brain: How the new science of consciousness explains our insatiable search for meaning.* New York: Basic Books.

Cameron, K. (2021). *Positively energizing leadership: Virtuous actions and relationships that create high performance.* Oakland: Berrett-Koehler.

Devis-Rozental, C. (2018). *Developing socio-emotional intelligence in higher education scholars.* London: Palgrave Macmillan.

Driscoll, J. (1994). Reflective practice for practise. *Senior Nurse,* 13, 47–50.

Dzulkifli, M. A. and Mustafar, M. F. (2013). The influence of colour on memory performance: A review. *The Malaysian Journal of Medical Sciences,* 20(2), 3–9.

Ellenbogen, J. M., Payne, J. D., and Stickgold, R. (2006). The role of sleep in declarative memory consolidation: Passive, permissive, active or none? *Current Opinion in Neurobiology,* 16(6), 716–722.

Exceptional Individuals. (2022). *Neurodiversity: Meanings, types & examples.* Available from: https://exceptionalindividuals.com/neurodiversity/ [Accessed 4 April 2022].

Fiorella, L. and Mayer, R. E. (2016). Eight ways to promote generative learning. *Educational Psychology Review,* 28, 717–741.

Gardner, H. E. (2000). *Intelligence reframed: Multiple intelligences for the 21st century.* London: Hachette.

Gibbs, G. (1988). *Learning by doing: A guide to teaching and learning methods.* Oxford: Further Education Unit.

Guilford, J. P. (1959). Three faces of intellect. *American Psychologist,* 14(8), 469–479.

Guilford, J. P. (1967). *The nature of human intelligence.* New York: McGraw-Hill Education.

Hussman, P. R. and O'Loughlin, V. D. (2018). Another nail in the coffin for learning styles? Disparities among undergraduate anatomy students' strategies, class performance, and reported VARK learning styles. *Anatomical Sciences Education,* 12(1), 6–19.

Lucas, B. and Claxton, G. (2010). *New kinds of smart: How the science of learnable intelligence is changing education.* Maidenhead: Open University Press.

McGee, P. (2016). *Hippo time is ok*. Available from: www.sumo4schools.com/the-six-sumo-principles/hippo-time-is-ok [Accessed 10 October 2022].

Negrete, A. (2020). Remembering rhythm and rhyme: Memorability of narratives for science communication. *Geoscience Communications*, 4(1), 1–9.

Nesbit, J. C. and Adelsope, O. O. (2006). Learning with concept and knowledge maps: A meta-analysis. *Review of Educational Research*, 76, 413–448.

Paas, F. and Sweller, J. (2012). An evolutionary upgrade of cognitive load theory: Using the human motor system and collaboration to support the learning of complex cognitive tasks. *Educational Psychology Review*, 24, 27–45.

Radović, T. and Dietrich, M. (2019). The impact of a mnemonic acronym on learning and performing a procedural task and its resilience toward interruptions. *Frontiers in Psychology*, 10(2522), 1–17.

Reddy, A. (2008). The eugenic origin of IQ testing: Implication for Post-Atkins litigation. *DePaul Law Review*, 667.

Robinson, K. and Aronica, L. (2009). *The element*. New York: Viking.

Robinson, R. (2016). *Divergent thinking Ken Robinson*. [YouTube]. Available from: www.youtube.com/watch?v=BHMUXFdBzik [Accessed 9 February 2021].

Rubin, D. C. (1998). *Memory in oral traditions: The cognitive psychology of epic ballads, and counting-out rhymes*. Oxford: Oxford University Press.

Scott, C. (2021). *Arts for health: Drawing*. Bingley: Emerald Publishing.

Tunku, S., Tunku, B., and Adawiah, D. (2013). The effect of humour and mood on memory recall. *Social and Behavioural Sciences*, 97(2013), 252–257.

Voss, P., Thomas, M. E., Cisneros-Franco, J. M., and de Villers-Sidani, É. (2017). Dynamic brains and the changing rules of neuroplasticity: Implications for learning and recovery. *Frontiers in Psychology*, 8, 1657.

Vredeveldt, A., Hitch, G. J., and Baddeley, A. D. (2011). Eye closure helps memory by reducing cognitive load and enhancing visualisation. *Memory & Cognition*, 39, 1253–1263.

Vygotsky, L. S. (1978). *Mind in society: The development of higher psychological processes*. Massachusetts: Harvard University Press.

Environmental wellbeing

Interacting with your surroundings

▶ INTRODUCTION

CONTENT WARNING

This chapter has content related to trauma and abuse that you may find triggering.

> "We are each other's environments".
>
> Denise Quinlan 2022

In this chapter, I will explore environmental wellbeing, with a focus on your university journey, from three perspectives based on Bronfenbrenner's bioecological model. The first relates to how the environment around you impacts your wellbeing, taking into account your physical surroundings and how these interact with you whilst impacting your sense of safety and the chance to flourish and thrive. The second explores how you can positively impact

DOI: 10.4324/9781003317548-6

your immediate environment by considering equity, diversity, inclusion and belonging. The third perspective looks further by exploring how, with your choices, you can make a positive impact on the world around you and how this, in turn, is also good for you. I will share the type of activities you can do and how these can have an overall positive impact. People sometimes think that their actions don't have an impact, but if you think about a pebble thrown into the sea, you will see that even though it is small, it will always make a ripple. When you start your university life, you will have new experiences, activities and surroundings that will inevitably have an impact on your life at that moment but also on the future.

As per previous chapters, within the various sections I will cover, there are activities and tips that you can put into practice to help you develop a better understanding of environmental wellbeing and indeed to improve it for your benefit but also for the benefit of others and of the world.

In this chapter, we will:

- Define environmental wellbeing
- Explore your external influences through Bronfenbrenner's bioecological model
- Explore how greener activities can have a positive impact on your wellbeing
- Explore your feeling of safety and environmental wellbeing, considering equity, diversity, inclusion and belonging
- Explore the importance of caring for your environment so it takes care of you
- Explore your impact on the environment
- Explore ways to improve your environmental wellbeing

Going to university presents an opportunity to learn new things, meet new people and try new experiences. This can be very exciting but also overwhelming, so preparing yourself for this by being aware of how your environment can affect you and how you can affect it can be useful.

▶ WHAT IS ENVIRONMENTAL WELLBEING?

According to Stride (2022), environmental wellbeing is "your sense of safety, comfort and connections with your physical surroundings". I would go further and say that it is also the sense of satisfaction and enjoyment that you get from making positive steps to impact your environment. It is about our relationship with the planet as well as with our immediate environment.

▶ YOUR EXTERNAL INFLUENCES: BRONFENBRENNER'S BIOECOLOGICAL MODEL

Another useful theory to think about ourselves and reflect on how we behave is by looking at Bronfenbrenner's (1977; Bronfenbrenner and Ceci 1994) bioecological model theory. Uri Bronfenbrenner (1977) was an American psychologist interested in child development. He developed a system looking at the multiple and multi-layered environmental aspects that could influence a child's development. He organised them into five interrelated categories in order of how much impact these will have on the child, with a child in the centre of the system and the nearest layer to the centre being the most influential.

One of the interesting things that have been overlooked until recently is how these systems that influenced the child can also be influenced by the child's behaviour and instigate change. Taking this into account, I have adapted his system to be used by adults and to get you to think about yourself and how external influences can impact your wellbeing and the ability to flourish but also how you can influence your environment with your actions, attitudes, behaviours, etc.

The five systems are: microsystem, mesosystem, exosystem, macrosystem and chronosystem. These are arranged in layers with the person in the centre, as you can see in Figure 6.1

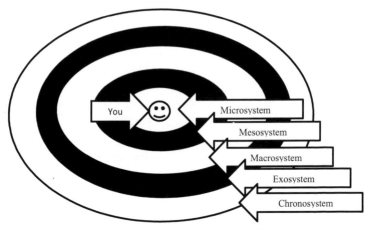

Figure 6.1 Layers in Bronfenbrenner bioecological system

Table 6.1 includes an explanation of each layer

TABLE 6.1 Bronfenbrenner bioecological model

Microsystem	The things/people that have a direct impact on you and that you can impact directly (your parents, siblings, partner, teachers, friends, the types of relationships you have)
Mesosystem	The things that interact or impact with those in your microsystem (your parents' friends, your school, your place of work, your partner's friends)
Exosystem	The external factors that influence the mesosystem (where you grew up, where you live, the media, your partner's place of work, social media)
Macrosystem	The cultural elements that can influence you (your beliefs, your culture, your ethnicity, your ideologies, your country)
Chronosystem	All the environmental changes that will happen during your life and impact on your ability to thrive (Covid-19, Brexit) but also those that include life-changing things (parents getting a divorce, moving to another country not by choice)

How can you use this model?

This model can be useful for getting you to think about the things in your life that have impacted how you behave, what you believe and why you are the way you are. It can help you challenge behaviours you are not happy about or get you to develop your thinking regarding important issues such as equity, diversity, inclusion or the environment. It can also be helpful for identifying how you have influenced those around you and if indeed this has transcended to the outer layers of the model.

Activity

To apply Bronfenbrenner's model to your life, you could ask yourself questions such as:

1. Do I treat people well?
2. Is the way I see people from other cultures influenced by my background?
3. Is behaving in this way helpful for my relationship? If not, why? And what can I do to change this behaviour?
4. What has gotten me to think this way?
5. Does this way of thinking help me develop meaningful relationships?
6. Am I being biased regarding these ideas? If yes, how?
7. Where do my values come from?
8. Do I feel comfortable with myself? If not, why?

There are many more questions you can ask yourself to grow, develop and improve your wellbeing. Still, even though some of the external factors happening around you will influence your experiences and your sense of identity, there are some that you cannot control, such as those in the outer system of the model; for example, your parents getting a divorce or the economic growth of the country. Even though these would most probably affect you, they cannot be changed, and worrying excessively about them can negatively impact your wellbeing.

This doesn't mean that you don't care; of course, we all have external things we care deeply about, but it is about finding the balance and being able to put them into context. That could also be said for the things that have happened in your past. They already have happened, and no amount of worrying about them will change them. We all have trauma to some extent. Some of us have been victims of abuse or seen terrible atrocities, and these will, of course, impact who we are. For those very difficult situations that linger on our mind and don't let us move on, it is key to seek support from a professional.

We should by no means deal with these by ourselves. Carrying all that pain is very bad for our wellbeing mentally, emotionally and even physically. However, moving on and letting go of those terrible experiences is liberating and a positive step towards a healthier life. Consequently, if we pay attention to the present and things that directly affect our experiences and behaviours, we will be more likely to make a positive impact on our wellbeing.

▶ YOUR ENVIRONMENT'S IMPACT ON YOUR WELLBEING

Your environment, the place where you spend your time, matters as it affects your wellbeing. What you see, hear and experience can impact your overall wellbeing. For example, if you spend too much time in a noisy environment, you may find that you are tense. Lighting, quality of air and temperature can also affect your wellbeing. For example, being in a small space which has restricted air could make you feel overwhelmed as you overheat.

Finding your happy place, where you feel safe, calm and able to be yourself, is an important aspect of environmental wellbeing. Keeping your room tidy, ensuring you keep your things in place and clean can also have a big impact on your wellbeing. It may not seem like it, but it really does, so it is important that you spend some time each week keeping up with your chores and ensuring your living space is clean and not cluttered. It may seem boring or tedious to even think about having to tidy up, but getting into the habit of doing it will help you in the long run. This is especially true if you live in student accommodation and share some of the areas with other people. You will need to ensure that you keep up with your "mess" so others don't get annoyed with you. However, it is even more important for you to keep your things tidy as this will help you concentrate better and feel good about yourself.

Here are ten useful tips to help you keep tidy:

1. Make it fun: put on your favourite music to get you in the mood for tidying, or make it into a fun game or a timed activity
2. Make a plan: setting aside a specific time during the week to do certain tasks can help you keep on top of them. This is also very useful if you are living with other students as you can agree on the rota of who does what and when.
3. Make it a routine: cleaning and tidying little and often will help you keep on top of things and won't be as overwhelming as if you have to spend hours doing it in one day
4. Double up: do some of your tidying whilst watching your favourite show. For example, you could fold your clothes whilst watching *Friends* for the umpteenth time. You probably know all the jokes by heart already.
5. Keep food out of your bed: avoid getting into the habit of eating in your bed. This will create a mess and make your bed very uncomfortable over time
6. Keep stuff in a dedicated space: make sure that your stationery is on your desk and your cutlery in your kitchen
7. Declutter: get rid of unnecessary things. If you don't need it, use it or enjoy it, chuck it. This also goes for checking the content of your fridge to make sure you are not letting things go off and waste.
8. You've got to wash up: if you are cooking you could wash what you have used as you go along. This will help you keep tidy and will make sure you stay in your roommate's good books. Also, get in the habit of washing your dishes as soon as you finish your food. That way, you or your roommate won't have to wake up to a dirty sink.

9. Make your bed: get in the habit of making your bed every morning. You will feel better for it.
10. Don't let your laundry pile up: set aside time every week, if you can, to wash your clothes

Student accommodation

As a student, it may be that you are staying home as you live near your chosen university. If this is the case and you are able, make sure you create a study space that is quiet and allows you to focus and concentrate. If you are moving to another area to study, you will probably need to rent a place. Most universities in the UK offer accommodation for first year students and for international students. This type of accommodation normally includes some of the bills (electricity, water, gas, Wi-Fi, for example). The type of accommodation you will get depends on your budget. Some may include catering (food), whilst others don't. Here are some types of accommodation that may be available to you:

- Flat (apartment)
  These are normally shared with other students (between six to ten depending on the size of the flat) and can be either en suite (with your own toilet and shower) or with shared toilets. In these flats, you share the kitchen and a communal area. Some buildings include common areas where you can study or socialise, as well as laundry spaces (the machines to wash and dry your clothes normally cost money to use).
- Studio
  Usually more expensive than flats, a studio gives you more privacy as you would have your own kitchenette and bathroom
- House/flat – share
  Usually houses or flats are shared between a number of students. Most of these are private rentals. Typically students have their own room but will have to share common areas such as the kitchen, lounge and usually the bathroom too.

Private renting is when you rent a flat/house or a room in one of these whilst sharing with others, not as part of the university accommodation but as a tenant from a landlord. This is more common for students after their first year when they must find their own accommodation. In this case, you can find a group of friends to share the rent with. These types of places don't always include the bills, so you must make sure you budget for these as part of your outgoings. Living with your friends can be great, providing you all agree on the house rules and understand that you are all responsible for any damages or unpaid bills.

Living with other people can be a fun way to create amazing memories, but remember to respect others' privacy and be mindful of how your attitude and actions can have an impact on other people. Get in the habit of washing your dishes as you use them, and leave shared spaces as you found them. Doing a rota can be a useful way to share spaces in harmony.

Spend time with nature

Research shows that being in nature can be great for us. It can reduce stress and even affect our immune system. Therefore, you should also plan every week, at least, to spend some time outdoors somewhere where you will find some nature. It can be a park, the beach, a forest or anything that you can access easily and probably freely. To make a positive impact on your environment, make sure you don't litter and consciously engage on keeping spaces clean and well kept. There's a saying about going to the beach and only leaving footprints; this should be the case for any outdoor environment.

Reduce your screen time

You should also make sure you limit your screen time, as spending too much time online or in front of a screen is detrimental to our mental and physical wellbeing. Screens have become part of our everyday lives, and it is difficult to stay away from them. We go from the phone screen to the laptop to the TV, but reducing our screen time can have a positive impact on our mental health.

Research shows that spending less time using our devices can lower stress, increase our self-esteem and even help us improve our relationships (Buabbas et al. 2021). Devices have ways to tell you the amount of time you spend on them, so you should make it a habit to check these. Other ways to reduce screen time are having a hobby, going outdoors, cooking a meal and spending time with friends or family. Practical things such as turning your device off overnight or keeping it away from your bed can also help.

When using devices, remember to take short, frequent breaks and stretch your body. I use a method in which I give myself a target; it could be a time target or a word count target if I am writing, and this helps me manage my screen time. What I do is I set the target; for example, "I am going to write 500 words today". Once I reach the word count, I stop, have a break, and if I still feel I can do a bit more, I do, but if I don't, it's fine. This helps me manage my deadlines and feel like I have achieved something. If you are using a device for browsing or social media, you could limit yourself by time and step away for a while to do something else. You will be surprised how much you can achieve in those spaces of time that you would normally be browsing. Your body and your mind will thank you for it.

Activity

Choose a week to pay attention to your environment and how it might be negatively affecting your wellbeing. Once you have done that, you should think about the changes you can make to your environment to have a positive impact on your wellbeing.

You can jot them down using Table 6.2

TABLE 6.2 Changing my environment to improve my wellbeing

Environment	Negative effect on my wellbeing	What can I do to change this?

▶ EQUITY, DIVERSITY, INCLUSION AND BELONGING

Taking into account that the environment and those around you influence you and you influence them, it is important to look at how we are treated and how we treat others. I wanted to do this through equity, diversity, inclusion and belonging, as these should be the basis from which we view others and ourselves.

Equality or equity?

Sometimes people confuse equality with equity, so it is important to define them so you can see where the difference lies. Equality is "ensuring that every individual has an equal opportunity to make the most of their lives and talents" (Equality and Human Rights Commission 2018). Notice here that there is an emphasis on giving everyone the same. That would mean the same treatment, the same support and the same education. There doesn't seem to be anything wrong with that at first glance.

However, do we all need and want the same? If that is the case, it would mean we have no individual needs. It would mean we all come from the same background, have the same privileges and are seen in the same way regardless of how we look like. We all know that is not the case; systems of oppression have ensured some of us are more privileged than others. In contrast, equity is giving people what they need in order to make things fair; not the same as everyone else but what THEY need. Each of us are in different circumstances, even if we are going through the same situations. For example, I am a wheelchair user, so I need to ensure that there are no steps wherever I go. You may not need that, so for you, that wouldn't be a problem. We are all different with different abilities, talents, level of education, cultural background and even different wishes, so getting what we specifically need would be much better than getting the same as everyone else that we may not need or may not meet our needs. For this reason, equity is a much better term to understand and apply.

Discrimination

Equity doesn't mean that people must be treated differently in a negative way, this is called discrimination, which is the unfair treatment of people based on certain characteristics. In fact, it is unlawful to discriminate against someone on the basis of certain characteristics. According to the Equality Act 2010 in the UK, these are the protected characteristics:

- Age
- Disability
- Gender reassignment
- Marriage and civil partnership
- Pregnancy and maternity
- Race
- Religion or belief
- Sex
- Sexual orientation

That means that anyone being discriminated on the basis of these protected characteristics is committing a crime and can be prosecuted.

We all belong to some of these groups and how we are treated and perceived will be, at times, based on these. But because we belong to many different groups depending on who we are, where we come from and what we do, these categories sometimes intersect.

Intersectionality

Intersectionality is the idea that systems of inequality based on protected characteristics and forms of discrimination cross over or combine to create specific forms of discrimination and or privilege. The term was coined by Kimberlé Crenshaw (1989) in her paper exploring the lack of intersection of race and sex when looking at black women's experiences.

Activity

To understand this better, let's reflect on your own identity.

Here are some questions to prompt you:

TABLE 6.3 Reflective questions about your self-identity

How old are you?

What is your gender?

Do you have a disability?

What is your sexual orientation?

Do you belong to a religion?
If yes, which one?

What is your race?

What is your ethnic background?

Do you consider yourself working
class, middle class, upper class?

Whatever you answered will be different from other people; this is your unique set of characteristics. And the experiences you will face will be informed and perhaps triggered by these, even if you don't want it or notice it.

Think about these two people:

TABLE 6.4 Example of intersectionality

Characteristic	Cate	Diego
Race	White	Black
Religion	Christian	Catholic
Gender	Female	Male
Sexual orientation	Gay	Gay
Class	Working class	Middle class

The experience of Cate, a white, working-class, gay, Christian woman, will not be the same as the experience of Diego, a black, middle-class, gay, Catholic man. They both have characteristics where they may experience discrimination, but their experiences differ. Cate may face discrimination for being a woman, for being gay, and perhaps for being working class too, whilst Diego may face discrimination for being black and gay. The reason why they may face discrimination for these characteristics and not the others is because there is a power imbalance. Women, people of colour and gay people have been oppressed, whilst characteristics such as middle class, white, Christian/Catholic or male haven't. These latter have traditionally held the power, at least in Western society.

Systems of oppression

Systems of oppression are discriminatory groups, institutions, norms, power structures that exist within society. All the "-isms" (racism, classism, sexism, ableism, etc.) are forms of oppression. In the context of social justice, oppression is discrimination against a social group that is backed by institutional power. That is to say, the various societal institutions such as culture, government, education, etc. are all complicit in the oppression of marginalized social groups while elevating dominant social groups.

Simon Fraser Public Interest Research Group (SFPIRG) 2020

There are many types of discrimination. I have summarised them in Table 6.5 with some examples.

Being discriminated against can impact someone's mental health and affect their lives in many ways. If you have never felt discriminated, you are privileged and should use that privilege by becoming an ally to support others so that they aren't discriminated against. That will be good for them but also for you since kindness, compassion and purpose are great for our wellbeing.

TABLE 6.5 Types of discrimination

Type of discrimination	Meaning	Example
Direct discrimination	Treating someone less favourably on the grounds of a protected characteristic	Natasha, a Polish woman is attending a job interview, and the interviewer makes fun of her accent. She doesn't get the job.
Indirect discrimination	Application of something to a whole group without considering specific needs (equality)	Not letting women play a game because the person organising the games thinks women are weaker
Associative discrimination	Direct discrimination against someone because they are linked to someone with a protected characteristic	Samuel is not invited to a party because their best friend is non-binary
Perceptive discrimination	Discrimination due to an assumption that the person has a protected characteristic	Lina, a cisgender woman, is not allowed to enter a bar because the doorman thinks she is a transgender woman
Harassment	Unacceptable behaviour which offends, insults, injures, threatens or demeans someone based on stereotypes	Every time Laura goes to get coffee, one of the customers makes her feel uncomfortable with innuendos and sexual comments
Bullying	Repetitively and intentionally hurting someone "where the relationship involves an imbalance of power. It can happen face to face or online" (ABA 2020).	Every time John goes to a lecture, there is a group of students who repeatedly make fun of his weight, call him names and ridicule him

Activity

Discrimination, prejudice, racism and other types of isms don't always happen due to bad intentions. Sometimes we make mistakes due to a lack of knowledge and understanding and may discriminate others without even realizing.

Read the different types of discrimination in Table 6.5, and reflect on each type of discrimination by answering the following questions:

TABLE 6.6 Reflection on discrimination

Question	Answer
Can you think of a time where you may have discriminated against someone?	Yes Please continue to the next question No That's great! Keep it up!
What happened? Why did you discriminate? Was it intentional or by accident?	
How do you think the person that you discriminated against felt?	
If you were in that situation again, what would you do?	

Words create worlds

Using discriminatory words in a colloquial manner (everyday language) normalises them and it reinforces the systems of oppression by directly or indirectly targeting marginalized groups.

- Types of unacceptable terminology
  - Racial: racist slurs
  - Homophobic: against gay people
  - Transphobic: against trans people
  - Misogynistic: against women
  - Ableist: against disabled people
  - Ageist: against someone's age
  - Xenophobic: against someone's country or culture
  - Antisemitic: against Jewish people
  - Islamophobic: against Muslim people

Banter or bullying

Banter is a British term that refers to a friendly and good-humoured exchange between people that know each other, where there is a playful interaction with jokes and harmless teasing. For it to be banter, everyone involved has to be in on the joke and find it funny and not offensive.

Banter becomes bullying when it becomes offensive, mean, unkind and when someone who is being targeted feels upset, embarrassed or humiliated and perhaps doesn't feel they can speak up (Service Complaints for the Ombudsman 2018).

Ditch the Label (2022) has a list of good suggestions that you can use to check your/others' banter. These are:

1. Keep it clear by not laughing at someone for any of their protected characteristics (basically, don't laugh at people; laugh with them)
2. If something is offensive and not funny, don't laugh; you will just encourage the bully, who is probably just seeking attention
3. If you see someone else not enjoying the banter, point it out, and challenge it as you would want someone else to do it if it was happening to you
4. Avoid highlighting something you know is a sensitive point for someone else; you know you wouldn't like that
5. Don't say it is "just banter" or "just kidding" when saying something hurtful

I would add:

To acknowledge when someone tells you that you have hurt them. Listen, apologise and change your behaviour so that doesn't happen again. And most importantly, always treat others as you would like them to treat you – with kindness and respect.

Privilege

As people become more aware of marginalisation, inequality and injustice, the notion of privilege and who has it has become quite common in our everyday language. Privilege is the advantage, benefit or right that a particular group in a society enjoys. We all have a certain amount of privilege depending on who we are, where we come from, what we do, what we look like and the situation we are in. To reflect on your privilege, I have adapted the privilege walk (Warwick Dean of Students Office 2020) for you to complete.

Activity

Let's think about privilege. Please complete the following exercise which I have adapted from the privilege walk activity widely available.

Now add up all the ticks; these are the privileges you have. Then add all the empty spaces; these are the areas where you may be marginalised. Nobody's walk will be the same, and some will have more privilege than others. If you do, make sure you use that privilege to support and uplift others.

However, if you are marginalised in many areas, you may wish to seek support. You are never alone. In the UK, the equality advisory support helpline (EASS) can help. www.equalityadvisoryser vice.com

Microaggressions

Microaggressions are subtle but hostile verbal, behavioural or environmental humiliations based on biased assumptions that are derogatory or negative towards others. There are many types of microaggressions based on someone's characteristics, like the ones we discussed previously in this chapter. Everyone makes assumptions based on their judgement, which may be biased based on our experiences or things we have learned. This is why it is important to reflect on our own biases, interactions and behaviours towards others. Microaggressions, much like bullying and other types of discrimination, can be harmful, even if unintended. If you commit a microaggression and someone calls you

TABLE 6.7 The privilege walk

Please add a tick for every statement that you identify with ✓
For example, in question one, if you don't have a disability, you
would add a tick; if you do, you would leave it blank

1. I don't have a disability

2. I have never felt uncomfortable about a joke related to my race, religion, ethnicity, gender, disability or sexual orientation but felt unsafe to confront the situation

3. I can go out holding the hand of my partner, and I'm not afraid that I will encounter violence because of our gender or sexual orientation

4. People always get my name right when I pronounce it

5. My parents have always told me that I am beautiful, smart and intelligent

6. My parent/s have good jobs

7. I never have to worry about which toilet to use

8. I never see members of my race, ethnic group, gender or sexual orientation portrayed on television in degrading roles

9. I have been offered a job or an opportunity because of my friend or family member

10. People always use my pronouns correctly (e.g. she, he, they)

11. My family has never had to move house because we couldn't afford the rent

12. I went to private school

13. English is my first language

14. One or both of my parents have a university degree

15. I usually work with people I feel are like me

16. I am able to move through the world without fear of sexual assault

17. I wouldn't think twice about calling the police if there's any trouble

18. I can go out without having to delegate caring responsibilities

19. I can buy new clothes without worrying about how I can afford them

20. I can walk home alone at night without any fear

21. I can go to any shop and find the hair and skin care products that match my skin and hair care needs

22. I have never suffered from mental illness

23. People never make fun of where I come from

24. People in my family don't suffer from mental illness

on it, apologise and learn from that experience so it doesn't happen again.

At the same time, microaggressions can happen to you, sometimes without you even noticing, but these can have an impact on your sense of self and, over time, affect the way you see and value yourself. If you feel you are the victim of a microaggression, here are some things you can do:

> **Decide whether you have the headspace to engage at this time.** It may be that you don't feel able or safe to call it out, and for your wellbeing, it might be better to let it be.
>
> **Stop the conversation, breathe in and try to stay calm.** Without accusation, **point out** how the comment/word/situation was not acceptable and how it made you feel. Do it firmly but kindly (they may have done it inadvertently).

If the other person responds well and apologises, congratulations! You just taught someone something important. If the person doesn't acknowledge your feelings or makes fun of you, walk away and ask yourself: do I need people like this in my life? Clearly this may be harder if it is a member of your family as you may not be able to stay away. Friends/family and those that know you well should respect you, and if they make a mistake, they probably would acknowledge it, especially if it hurts you. If they don't, you may want to find the right time to have a chat so that they can see your point of view and how their behaviour or action is harmful.

We are all constantly learning and developing our understanding, and change takes time, so be patient if you can, unless you feel unsafe; in which case, seek support.

Here are some examples of microaggressions. I have left the last column empty so you can reflect on how the person may feel:

TABLE 6.8 Understanding microaggressions

Microaggression	Target	Possible bias	The person may feel . . .
"What she is trying to tell you is . . ."	Women	Sexism	
"You still have an accent".	Someone whose first language is not the one they are speaking	Xenophobia	
"You are not sick, you look normal".	Disabled person	Ableism	
"You are too old to understand this".	Older people	Ageism	
"I don't see colour. You look the same as me".	A person of colour	Racism	
You are only gay because you haven't met the right woman yet".	Gay people	Homophobia	

Diversity

Diversity refers to any characteristic that differentiates groups and people from one another. It means respect for and appreciation of differences. But it's more than this. We all bring with us diverse perspectives, work experiences, lifestyles and cultures. The power of diversity is unleashed when we respect and value differences. Diversity is defined by who we are as individuals.

- Types of diversity:
  - Ability/disability
  - Gender
  - Sexual orientation

- Age
- Ethnicity
- Race
- Religion
- Culture
- Class
- Education

If you completed the privilege walk, you may already be aware of your privilege but also of how different you are from anyone else. Valuing diversity is about recognising, welcoming and celebrating our many differences, learning from others and always respecting them. As I have said in a previous chapter, we are as unique as a fingerprint, inimitable and amazing; that's something to celebrate! We live in a multicultural world, and globalisation has opened opportunities for all of us to learn from others and to experience different cultures. Here is a list of some things you can do to promote diversity:

- Read books from authors from different backgrounds, ethnicities or cultures
- Learn to pronounce other people's names correctly
- Listen to music from different backgrounds and cultures
- Be open to learning from others
- Be curious about other people's cultures with respect and empathy
- Listen to other people's lived experiences

The following model can be useful to understand where you are in your journey to embrace and learn from other cultures.

The developmental model of intercultural sensitivity

This model developed by Bennett (2013) is one of the most influential models when talking about intercultural communication. It describes the ways in which people experience, interpret and interact across cultures considering cultural differences.

The model presents the idea that as our experience of cultural differences become more complex, our competence on how to manage those experiences will increase. Basically, the more we learn about different cultures, the more able we will be to find commonalities and embrace differences. The more we learn and expose ourselves to different cultures, ways of thinking and being and any other differences within cultures, the better and more open we will become to understand them and to explore them.

This reminds me of the notion of the echo chamber, which is an environment where we are only exposed to the same ways of being and thinking, and therefore these ideas are reinforced as the whole truth. Sometimes our social media can be an echo chamber, depending on what we like and follow. This can be dangerous as it doesn't expose us to different ways of being and may make our ideas narrow and our assumptions superficial.

> By identifying and recognising how we currently experience cultural differences, we can develop our understanding and seek to develop it to be fully inclusive.
>
> The model goes from ethnocentrism, which is when we experience our own experience as the key to our reality, to ethnorelativism, which is the experience of our own culture and that of others as relative to its context. This may seem a bit complex, but basically, it is the idea that there is a spectrum from believing that your reality is the only real one to understanding that your experience is expanded when it considers other points. In between these, there are six stages which are:
>
> - Denial: when an individual thinks their experience is the only real one
> - Defence: when an individual thinks their experience is the only good one, creating a them and us culture
> - Minimisation: when an individual thinks that there experience is the one everyone else has
> - Acceptance: when an individual thinks that their experience is one of many equally complex ways to view the world

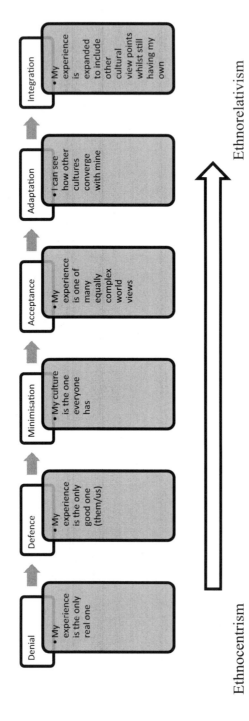

Figure 6.2 The development model of intercultural sensitivity (Bennett 2013)

- Adaptation: When an individual thinks that their culture and that of others converge with theirs whilst being different
- Integration: when an individual thinks that their experience is expanded to include other cultural points of view whilst still having their own

In an ideal world, everyone would be in the integration stage, and we could all live in peace, celebrating our similarities as well as our differences and being able to understand other people's point of view and to learn from them as much as they would learn from us. The reality is that this is quite difficult, especially in a polarised world where people are divided in fundamental ways and are not willing to compromise, learn or explore others' views. This model is important as you get ready for university or work as you will enter multicultural environments where you will be exposed to different experiences, ideas and ways of being and behaving that may not be familiar to you.

Activity

Reflection and action

Learning about this model presents you with an opportunity for growth and to develop an open mind. Think about a topic/belief/idea that you feel strongly about, and go through the model of intercultural sensitivity to identify where you are at. This will help you think about what you can do to get to the next stage. Some areas to consider could be religion, political views, sustainability, race, ethnicity, rights or any others where you feel you need to check yourself on. If you feel you are in the integration step, that's great! Perhaps you can think of another topic to check that one out too. If you find yourself leaning towards ethnocentrism, don't feel worried or guilty, but rather see it as an opportunity to take yourself out of your comfort zone and learn about yourself and others.

The idea here is to challenge your biased views and be open to learning from others whilst staying true to your values and beliefs. In Chapter 7, I explore values in more depth.

Inclusion

The definition of inclusion is the practice or policy of providing "opportunities and resources for people who might otherwise be excluded or marginalized" (Oxford Languages 2020). Being inclusive is about embracing others and being embraced by others without bias, judgement or preconceptions. Even if we are from a marginalized group, there are always things we can do to engage others to become more inclusive or to become more inclusive ourselves. Here are some examples:

- Learning or teaching in safe but uncomfortable spaces
- Creating spaces where you and others can explore biases safely
- Actively becoming advocates or allies
- Listening to other marginalised groups
- Amplifying the voices of other marginalised groups
- Apologising if you feel you haven't been inclusive
- Calling it out if you see someone not being included or you feel you have been excluded
- Challenging those who discriminate if it is safe to do so
- Being a role model, embodying the attitudes and behaviours that include others

How lucky are we?

When I was researching for this topic, I found this list which really puts things into perspective. It was developed by the Red Cross (2018).

Of course, this is not to say that because you are lucky in some or all these things, everything is always okay. Experiences change constantly, and there may be times where you go through difficult situations However, it is also important to develop gratitude and appreciation for the good things in life that we have or that happen to us. After all, gratitude is great for your wellbeing.

TABLE 6.9 The lucky ones

If you woke up this morning with more health than illness . . .	. . . then you are luckier than the million who will not survive this week
If you have never experienced the danger of battle, the loneliness of imprisonment, the agony of torture or the pangs of starvation . . .	. . . then you are ahead of 500 million people in the world
If you can attend any meeting you want – political, religious, social . . .	. . . then you are luckier than three billion people in the world
If you have food in the refrigerator, clothes on your back, a roof over your head and a place to sleep . . .	. . . then you are richer than 75% of this world
If you have money in the bank, in your wallet and spare change in a dish someplace . . .	. . . then you are among the top 8% of the world's wealthy
If you can read a list like this list . . .	. . . then you don't belong to the one billion people who CANNOT read

Belonging

Belonging is an innate need that we all have to be accepted, respected and supported. The idea of being a part of something bigger than us and feeling we are making a meaningful contribution to that community. Feeling part of a family, a group of friends, a class, a university, a religion, a sport can all help us feel that we belong. People that have a sense of belonging have higher levels of wellbeing and overall satisfaction.

When you start university and arrive in a new place where you have to start fresh and make new friends, possibly be away from home for the first time and are in a new environment, you may feel out of place or that you don't belong. That is completely normal, and developing that sense of belonging may take time. This will also be the case for those around you. You should remember that most of your classmates are doing something new for the first time too. That doesn't mean that you will all have the same experience. Some will fit in straight away, whilst others will take more time before they find their place. There are some things you can do to foster a sense of belonging in yourself and others. Here are some examples:

- Be open-minded and make an effort without compromising your values
- Set boundaries and surround yourself with people you feel safe to be yourself
- Be observant of other people's feelings, and include them if you can
- Be accepting, kind, respectful and considerate
- Be a role model for the way you would like to be treated
- Take time to develop friendships
- Develop your self-awareness so you know your limits
- Be curious, ask people about themselves
- Listen more
- Find things in common with others

Remember, we are all different and have different needs, but we also have a lot of things in common, and feeling valued, respected, supported and that we belong is something we all want and need to flourish.

Activity

Lived experiences: think about the individuals in Table 6.10 as if they were one of your classmates, taking into account their protected characteristics. Reflect on their experience and how you would behave to support them so they feel included, appreciated and respected.

▶ CARING FOR YOUR ENVIRONMENT

Reduce, reuse, repair, rethink, recycle – these are the five Rs that will help you take care of your environment. Global warming,

TABLE 6.10 Exploring lived experiences

Classmate	What barriers might they face?	What can a university/ employer do to support them?	Which microaggressions should they and you be aware of?	What could you do to make this person feel included?
Peter is a white, British, cisgender man. He is blind. He attended a state school and is the only person in his family to attend university. Peter's parents struggle financially, so he has taken on a part-time job whilst at university.				
Milena is a white, Polish, cisgender woman. She grew up in care but was adopted when she was 14 and attended a private school. Her adoptive parents help her with some of the costs related to university life. Milena has a part-time job as she likes to have financial independence.				
Andy is a white, Jewish, nonbinary person. They attended a grammar school. They have social anxiety. Their parents are middle class and can help with their university accommodation fees. Andy's parents are very supportive of their choices.				
Maria is an international student from Mexico who won a scholarship to study in the UK. She is a Black, cisgender, gay woman who lives with her girlfriend. Maria is not in contact with her parents as they don't approve of her sexuality. Her partner works part time, and money is tight.				
Michael is an Afro-Caribbean, cisgender man. He is a mature student who is married and has two children under the age of three. He went to state school and had to leave at 16 to find work. Michael has a part-time job in a bar, and his wife stays at home looking after the children. Michael sometimes has to use crutches as he has chronic pain in his knee.				

unethical farming, corporate social responsibility, sustainability and other terms have in the past decade become increasingly important as we become more aware of our impact on our planet. This can be overwhelming if we feel a sense of responsibility to the planet. And although we may not be able to change the world's fate, there are things you can do that, whilst small, can make a difference. Here are some examples:

Can you think of any other things you can do to help the environment?

TABLE 6.11   Making a positive impact on your environment

Reduce	• By protecting natural resources by saving on electricity and water, only using what you need and unplugging electronic items or even lowering the central heating. If you are living in university accommodation in the UK, electricity and water bills may be included in your rent; however, private accommodation normally doesn't, so being aware of your electricity and water usage can also be good for your wallet. • By reducing meat consumption even if you are not vegan or vegetarian is good for the environment and also for your finances as meat tends to be more expensive • By using less paper, only printing what you need • By saving on fuel by cycling or walking, if you are able, or sharing a lift with a friend • By using energy-efficient bulbs
Reuse	• By using reusable bags • By using plastic bottles and other items • By using mugs to get your coffee
Repair	• Your clothes • Technology
Rethink	• Where you shop, making sure it is ethical • Where you travel to • Shopping local if you can • The choices you make and the impact these can have on your environment, others and yourself
Recycle	• By buying second-hand items such as clothes, furniture, a bicycle, for example • By following the local guidelines for recycling materials

Being aware of your choices and their impact is important. At university, you can make an impact by being aware of their sustainability guidance and by being respectful of their environment. You can go further by engaging with your university or student union to be an activist and role model, making suggestions and campaigns to improve their sustainability.

Terminology matters

Considering that words create worlds and that they can be powerful to the giver and the receiver, it is important that we understand and use terminology correctly and respectfully. Here are some words that we have explored within this chapter with their definitions.

Ally: advocates for people from underrepresented or marginalized groups. An ally takes action to support people outside of their own group.

Cisgender: a term used to describe people whose gender identity matches the sex they were assigned at birth. Often abbreviated as cis.

Corporate social responsibility: practicing good corporate citizenship by going beyond profit maximization to make a positive impact on communities and societies

Emotional tax: the combination of being on guard to protect against bias, feeling different at work because of gender, race and/ or ethnicity and the associated effects on health, well-being and ability to thrive at work

Intersectionality: the intertwining of social identities such as gender, race, ethnicity, social class, religion, sexual orientation and/or gender identity, which can result in unique experiences, opportunities and barriers

Neurodiverse: the concept that there is great diversity in how people's brains are wired and work, and that neurological differences should be valued in the same way we value any other human variation

Non-binary: a category for a fluid constellation of gender identities beyond the woman/man gender binary

Unconscious bias: an implicit association about a person based on mistaken or inaccurate information

▶ OVERVIEW

Taking care of our environment so it takes care of us is a priority. Our world needs us to be aware of how our actions and our choices have consequences. In this chapter, I have explored environmental wellbeing from various aspects to get you to reflect on these. Ultimately, the choices you make are yours. I hope you have found the ideas, activities and knowledge I have shared useful. These are the main things we covered in this chapter:

• Define environmental wellbeing
• Explore your external influences through Bronfenbrenner bio-ecological model
• Explore how greener activities can have a positive impact on your wellbeing
• Explore your feeling of safety and environmental wellbeing considering equity, diversity, inclusion and belonging
• Explore the importance of caring for your environment so it takes cares of you
• Explore your impact on the environment
• Explore ways to improve your environmental wellbeing

▶ REFERENCES

Aba (Anti bullying alliance). (2020). *Definition of bullying.* Available from: www.anti-bullyingalliance.org.uk/tools-information/all-about-bullying/what-bullying/aba-definition-bullying [Accessed 20 November 2020].

Bennett, M. (2013). *Basic concepts of intercultural communication: Paradigms, principles, & practices*. Boston: Intercultural Press.

Bronfenbrenner, U. (1977). Toward an experimental ecology of human development. *American Psychologist*, 32(7), 513.

Bronfenbrenner, U. and Ceci, S. J. (1994). Nature-nurture reconceptualised: A bio-ecological model. *Psychological Review*, 10(4), 568–586.

Buabbas, A. J., Hasan, H., and Buabbas, M. A. (2021). The associations between smart device use and psychological distress among secondary and high school students in Kuwait. *PLoS One*, 16(6), e0251479. https://doi.org/10.1371/journal. pone.0251479.

Crenshaw, K. (1989). Demarginalizing the intersection of race and sex: A black feminist critique of antidiscrimination doctrine, feminist theory and antiracist politics. *University of Chicago Legal Forum* (1), 139–167.

Ditch the Label. (2022). *Banter or bullying*. Available from: www.ditch thelabel.org/banter-or-bullying/ [Accessed 6 July 2022].

Equality and Human Rights Commission. (2018). *Understanding equality*. Available from: www.equalityhumanrights.com/en/secondary-education-resources/useful-information/understanding-equality [Accessed 10 October 2020].

Oxford Languages. (2020). *Inclusivity*. Available from: https://languages. oup.com/google-dictionary-en/ [Accessed 10 November 2020].

Quinlan, D. (2022). *Collective resilience: Resilience grows between you as well as within you*. Available from: https://nziwr.co.nz/collective-resi lience-resilience-grows-between-you-as-well-as-within-you/ [Accessed 1 December 2022].

Red Cross. (2018). *Lucky ones*. Available from: www.redcross.ca/crc/docu ments/What-We-Do/Emergencies-and-Disasters-WRLD/educa tion-resources/lucky_ones_povdisease.pdf [Accessed 17 November 2020].

Service Complaints for the Ombudsman. (2018). *Banter or bullying – how can you tell the difference?* Available from: www.scoaf.org. uk/2018/03/19/march-2018-banter-or-bullying-how-can-you-tell-the-difference/ [Accessed 20 November 2020].

Simon Fraser Public Interest Research Group (SFPIRG). (2020). *Systems of oppression*. Available from: https://sfpirg.ca/infohub/systems-of-oppression/ [Accessed 23 November 2020].

Strides. (2022). *Environmental wellness*. Available from: https://stride. com.au/dimensions-of-wellness/environmental-wellness/ [Accessed 5 July 2022].

Warwick Dean of Students Office. (2020). *Privilege walk*. Available from: https://warwick.ac.uk/services/dean-of-students-office/community-values-education/educationresources/privilegewalk/instructions_ for_running_the_privilege_walk [Accessed 29 October 2020].

7 Occupational wellbeing

Finding your purpose

▶ **INTRODUCTION**

In this chapter, I will explore the concept of occupational wellbeing, which is related to your attitude towards your work. This is a type of wellbeing that sometimes is overlooked, especially if you are starting your university journey. It may be that you don't really want to think about what you want to do in the future. Or it may also be that you already know what you want to do. Or it could even be that what you want to do in the future is all you think about, and you would like to get there pretty fast. Wherever you feel you are, this chapter will be useful to help you in your quest, as I will explore it from a personal perspective considering your strengths, values and ideals, which can be useful if you already know what you want but can also be helpful even if you don't.

One thing that is important to consider is that career paths have changed. By this, I mean that we live in an ever-changing world where you will need to be adaptable, flexible and able to cope with change. Unlike in the previous generations, where people would stay in one profession or one job for most of their working life, current employment trends show that individuals change jobs and even industries many times. This could be due to many

DOI: 10.4324/9781003317548-7

reasons, such as a lack of job satisfaction or career advancement. But it is also a reality due to changing work environments. If you think about it, some of the jobs that exist now didn't exist 20 years ago. With technological advances, changes in working patterns and the emergent working-from-home trend due to Covid-19, it is difficult to predict the jobs that will be available in the future.

For this reason, this chapter is not about finding what your job should be but rather finding your talents, values, strengths and creativity so that you can fit these into whichever job you want to do.

Within this chapter, as in previous chapters, I have included exercises, reflections and activities for you to explore this dimension of wellbeing.

These are the main areas we will explore:

- What is occupational wellbeing?
- How your personal values matter
- The importance of knowing your character strengths
- Finding your element to help you thrive
- Being in the zone to perform at your best
- The notion of creativity and how you can exercise it
- Finding your purpose and identifying the things you love to do to help you live your best life

▶ WHAT IS OCCUPATIONAL WELLBEING?

Occupational wellbeing is the attitude you have towards your work. It considers the satisfaction you get from doing something and the opportunities to use your strengths whilst doing it. It is about finding what you love to do and the things that align with your values and pursuing these. Occupational wellbeing considers a healthy work-life balance, the ability to manage stress in your workplace and the opportunities to develop meaningful relationships with the people you work with. I have covered some of these areas in previous chapters, so I will focus on those

I haven't covered. These areas are also relevant to your university journey as you will have to work with others, manage stress and, most importantly, learn about yourself.

One thing that I feel strongly about occupational wellbeing is that it shouldn't be focused only on paid employment. There are many ways to be fulfilled. For some people, fulfilment will come from the job they do, but for others, fulfilment will come from doing other things like volunteering, arts and crafts, etc. To be able to do those things, they may need a job that, although not bringing them fulfilment or a sense of purpose, allows them the space to pursue other things they like to do. You need to find what works for you and what sits well with your values.

▶ YOUR PERSONAL VALUES

Values are those things that are important to you and that guide your behaviour, ideas and attitudes. They are the foundation of your beliefs and are linked to your sense of self: the way you see yourself and who you are. Your values are, in a sense, your internal compass guiding you to what feels right for you. They are influenced by your culture, family, upbringing, environment and even friends.

When the way you or others act aligns with your values, you will feel satisfied and at ease. However, when your attitude or behaviour or that of others doesn't align with your values, you will feel uncomfortable and unhappy. For example, honesty is one of my top values, so when someone lies to me, I feel very let down.

Activity

Identifying your values

For this activity, you should identify your five most important values.

1. Below I have included a list of values. Read them, thinking about yourself, and choose the five that most align with your beliefs.

This may be quite difficult to begin with, so if you are not sure about what your values are, here are some prompts to get you thinking about them:

- What is important to you?
- What type of behaviour makes you angry or sad?
- When do you feel happiest?
- What type of behaviour makes you feel good?
- What makes you proud?
- What would you love to do if money or time were not an issue?

2. You can start by choosing around 20 and then narrowing it down until you find the five that most matter to you.

List of values adapted from Brené Brown's website (brenebrown. com 2022):

Accountability
Achievement
Adaptability
Adventure
Altruism
Ambition
Authenticity
Balance
Beauty
Belonging
Caring
Collaboration
Commitment
Compassion
Competence
Confidence
Connection
Contentment
Contribution
Cooperation
Courage
Creativity
Curiosity

Dignity
Diversity
Environment
Efficiency
Equality
Ethics
Excellence
Fairness
Faith
Family
Financial stability
Forgiveness
Freedom
Friendship
Generosity
Giving back
Grace
Gratitude
Growth
Happiness
Harmony
Health
Home
Honesty
Hope
Humility
Humour
Inclusion
Independence
Integrity
Intuition
Job security
Justice
Kindness
Knowledge
Leadership
Learning
Love
Loyalty

Making a difference
Nature
Openness
Optimism
Order
Patience
Peace
Peace of mind
Perseverance
Power
Pride
Recognition
Reliability
Respect
Responsibility
Risk-taking
Safety
Security
Self-discipline
Self-expression
Self-respect
Service
Simplicity
Spirituality
Sportsmanship
Success
Teamwork
Time
Tradition
Trust
Truth
Understanding
Uniqueness
Usefulness
Vision
Vulnerability
Wealth
Wellbeing
Wisdom

Can you think of any other values that you feel are important?

3. Once you have identified the five values that matter to you the most, ask yourself:
   - Do I live by these values every day?
   - How do I feel when I do?
   - How do I feel when I don't?
   - How can I continue living by these values?

Now that you have identified your core values, let's look at your character strengths.

▶ CHARACTER STRENGTHS

Character strengths are the positive characteristics that you express through your thoughts, feelings and behaviours (Peterson and Seligman 2004). Working to your strengths can make your life more fulfilled and help you grow and flourish. According to Quinlan and Hone (2021, p. 96), "character strengths and wellbeing are malleable" and can be developed with practice.

> You have the power to positively influence your wellbeing by focusing on your highest character strengths. Research shows that if you have an active awareness of your character strengths you are nine times more likely to flourish.
> VIA Institute of Character 2020

Peterson and Seligman (2004) developed the VIA classification of strengths where they identified and grouped the virtues we have to help us lead a better life. After extensive research, they came up with six core virtues and 24 character strengths.

- Wisdom and knowledge: cognitive character strengths related to gaining and using knowledge
  - Creativity: thinking of new ways of doing things
  - Curiosity: showing an interest in experiences
  - Love of learning: enjoying gaining new skills and knowledge
  - Perspective: being able to see the bigger picture

- Courage: emotional character strengths
  - Bravery: being able to face problems or challenges or standing for what you believe
  - Perseverance: seeing things through
  - Honesty: being genuine and truthful
  - Zest: tackling life with excitement and energy
- Humanity: interpersonal character strengths to cultivate meaningful relationships
  - Love: valuing your relationships and demonstrating warmth
  - Kindness: being friendly, caring and compassionate to others
  - Social intelligence: understanding others
- Justice:
  - Teamwork: working well with others
  - Fairness: treating others impartially and justly
  - Leadership: supporting and engaging others to make things happen
- Temperance:
  - Forgiveness: letting go of resentment
  - Humility: being humble about your achievements
  - Prudence: thinking before acting/speaking
  - Self-regulation: being able to manage your emotions and behaviours
- Transcendence:
  - Appreciation of beauty and excellence: being responsive in a positive way to the world around you
  - Gratitude: feeling of thankfulness for things in life
  - Hope: expecting positive things to happen
  - Humour: finding the funny or lighter side of life
  - Spirituality: finding meaning and purpose beyond yourself

We are all capable of having these character strengths to some extent. These are malleable, and your highest strengths, which are your top five, are called signature strengths and can change depending on your environment and circumstances. When we use our signature strengths, we may feel:

- Energised and excited
- A sense of intrinsic motivation to use that strength
- Authenticity
- Wanting to use the strength

TABLE 7.1 Reflecting on your character strengths

Signature strengths	How can I continue strengthening my strengths whilst living by my values?

If you want to find out what your top character strengths are, you can do so by going to www.viacharacter.org/character-strengths (VIA Institute of Character 2020), where you will be invited to take a free survey and you will receive a report with your strengths.

Activity

If you have identified your top strengths, do they relate to the values you identified in the previous section?

In this activity, you can reflect on how you can continue strengthening your signature strengths, taking into account your values.

▶ FINDING YOUR ELEMENT

Living a fulfilled life where you are doing things you are good at and things you enjoy is important for your occupational wellbeing. Sir Ken Robinson, the renowned educationalist who criticized the current educational methods for squashing creativity, defined "the element" as that point where the things we are good at and the things we love to do come together. We all may have many

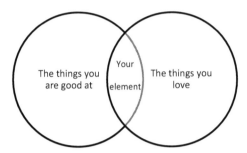

Figure 7.1 Finding your element

elements, and these may change throughout our lives depending on our circumstances. We are in a constant state of growth, development and possibilities.

Robinson argued that finding your element is key to your wellbeing but also to making a positive impact on your community. To find your element, there are two main features that need to be present and two main conditions to enable it.

Features

1. Aptitude/talents
   Your natural abilities: those things that, while others may find difficult to do, you can do with ease and without effort. It could be anything: singing, running, writing, doing maths; it doesn't matter what it is as long as it comes natural to you. Having a mentor may help you find your aptitudes.
2. Passion
   Those things that when you do them, they give you great pleasure and joy

Conditions

1. Attitude
   An optimistic perspective, how you see yourself, self-belief, perseverance and motivation. This links to work we discussed

in previous chapters around a positive mindset and socio-emotional intelligence. People with this attitude are more likely to achieve more.

2. Opportunity

Seeking situations where you can practice your aptitudes in various ways

According to Robinson and Aronica (2009) there are three main limitations to finding your element, and these are:

- Not understanding your capacities for intelligence, feeling, imagination, physical awareness or intuition
- Not understanding how these capacities are related
- Not realising your potential to grow and develop. This would link to having a growth mindset, something I discussed in Chapter 5.

These three limitations are influenced by the way you see yourself, by your culture, your background, your mental health and by those around you. So how can you find your aptitudes? If you completed the activities to find your values and your character strengths, you are on your way to finding your element. Becoming more self-aware by practicing some of the activities dotted within this book can also help you find your element.

Why does finding your element matter?

There are three main reasons why finding your element matters. These are:

- Personal so you get to know yourself better and what you are able to do well
- Social so you have a purpose in life, something that research shows is key to your wellbeing
- Economic so you can find a profession that you love and gives you the life you want

How do you know when you are in your element?

When you are in your element, when doing an activity, you will feel more energised, more enthusiastic and motivated. When you are not in your element, you may feel tired, bored or even moody, and if you feel like this, you need to tune into yourself and check in to see why you are feeling like that and what can be done to stop feeling like that. Be curious about yourself, your likes and dislikes. Richard Gerver (2016), a renowned educator, talks about being open-minded and willing to challenge our thinking and see curiosity as a habit we should all practice every day.

▶ BEING IN THE ZONE (EN TU SALSA)

There is a saying in Spanish for when you are totally immersed in an activity. The feeling when you are completely in the moment, performing at your best and doing what you absolutely love. When you lose the concept of time, of your surroundings and even when hunger, frustrations, sadness and anything in between just disappear. We call this "estar en tu salsa" – "to be in your sauce", and Robinson calls this "being in the zone" – the deep heart of the element. Being in the zone feels amazing, and it requires a lot of energy, but it isn't something we should aim to feel all the time. Resting, recharging and doing nothing are also important aspects of wellbeing.

How do you know when you are in the zone?

Robinson argues that when you feel a sense of freedom and are being your authentic self, doing something you love and are naturally good at, feeling you are living your truth and doing what you are meant to be doing, that's when you are in the zone. Gerver (2016, agreeing with this, adds that authenticity and passion are key to being successful, perhaps because when you are at your best, you are being authentic and passionate. Furthermore, to achieve this, you need to be dedicated enough and create the right environment to enable that to happen. It could be that once you have created the conditions to let your authentic self be, you will be in the zone. Being in the zone makes time feel as if it is going by faster, while being bored or not engaged makes it feel slower. Being in the zone makes you more creative, and ideas flow faster and easier.

Other researchers call being in the zone "flow", a term developed by Csikszentmihalyi (2002) to describe the moment when you are so focused on doing something you love that nothing else matters; the space where you lose yourself in the activity, giving it all your attention and, concurring with Robinson, where time is distorted. His work adds the idea of enjoyment to have this optimal experience as key, basically having fun whilst you are doing it. Activities we love to do give us energy. "If you're doing something that you love, by the end of the day you may be physically tired but spiritually energized"(Robinson and Aronica 2009, p. 92). Experiencing flow or being in the zone helps us feel connected with our sense of self, but it also impacts our body, as when we are in flow, our body releases endorphins, dopamine and adrenaline, and even our breathing and heart rate can change.

While "being in the zone"/"in your element" is great and something anyone can experience if you have ADHD (attention deficit hyperactivity disorder) or OCD (obsessive compulsive disorder) you may find yourself regularly hyper focusing on a project or task without eating or drinking all day, and this can affect your ability to carry out other daily activities (Ashinoff and Abu-Akel 2021). This fixation can have a detrimental effect on your wellbeing and is not the purpose of being in the zone, and it may then be something to speak about with a professional.

Finding your people to share your talents with

When you are in your element, you may feel more able to connect with others who share your passion, and this will make you feel comfortable to be your true self, genuine and inimitable. So finding your people is a good way to find and share your element. We all have different talents, and that makes us very special. Sharing your talent with the world, whatever it is, will enrich it as there is nobody else in the whole world with your exact talent.

How to find your element?

The most important thing is to be willing to look for it within yourself. Spend time with yourself, turning down the distractions around you and thinking about what you like, what you love, what you are good at and what you are not so good at. Be open to new ideas, and be curious about yourself and the world around you. Have a positive attitude by exploring what could be possible and creating opportunities to find your talents. Once you think you know what your element is, you should find your clan, those who share your passion, and share it together. Being proactive and making things happen is also key to finding your element.

Activity

Finding your element

In this section, you will complete four steps to help you find your element.

1. Make a list of your strengths and weaknesses

TABLE 7.2 Strengths and weaknesses

Strengths	Weaknesses

2. Go over your strengths, and check which of these make you feel joyful, and make a note of which ones these are

TABLE 7.3 Strengths that make me happy

Strengths that make me happy

3. Identify any other ideas, activities or situations that make you joyful

TABLE 7.4 Things that give me joy

Things that give me joy

4. Reflect on your strengths and the things that give you joy
   a. How much do you use them?
   b. When do you use/do them?
   c. When don't you use/do them?
   d. Why don't you use/do them?
   e. How can you use/do them more?

Now that you have reflected on your strengths and the things that make you happy, you may have a better idea of how to use these more to find your element.

▶ THE IMPORTANCE OF CREATIVITY

"You can't be a creative thinker if you're not stimulating your mind, just as you can't be an Olympic athlete if you don't train regularly".

Sir Ken Robinson

Surprisingly for some, creativity is something that can be learned, and that should be practiced to strengthen. Some people think they

TABLE 7.5 Imagination, creativity and innovation

Imagination	Creativity	Innovation
When you can step outside of your current state When you can think of the past or the future When you put yourself in someone else's shoes (empathise)	When you have original ideas that have value When you do something about it (active) When you have a process of: trial and error When original thinking happens in the moment	When you apply your creativity to create something new When you develop something novel that is of use

are not creative because they can't do art. That is inaccurate; whenever you are solving a problem, finding a solution, coming up with an idea or exploring things from a different perspective, you use your creativity. Creativity is important. According to the World Economic Forum (2020), creativity is a very important skill alongside complex problem-solving and critical thinking. "With the avalanche of new products, new technologies, and new ways of working, workers are going to have to become more creative in order to benefit from these changes." Research by LinkedIn learning concluded that "creativity is the most important skill in the world" (Petrone 2018).

So, if you are going to need to be creative in the workplace, it makes sense to practice creativity at university too. According to Robinson (2001), imagination, creativity and innovation are closely linked. Robinson and Robinson (2022, p. 13) tell us that "it is through imagination that we create the worlds in which we live. We can also re-create them". Innovation is the source of creativity, and creativity is putting your imagination to work. Innovation happens when your creativity allows you to put those good ideas into practice.

Activities to exercise your creativity

- Learn something new like a language, an instrument, a song or even a new topic
- Practice your skills on a regular basis
- Challenge yourself to try something new or go the extra mile

- Meet new people, and be curious about them
- Look at things from a different perspective
- Read something different to what you usually read
- Let you mind wander freely
- Practice analysing, evaluating and exploring topics
- Play more
- Question yourself often
- Create a vision board for your goals
- Put yourself in someone else's shoes
- Role play
- Try new things
- Write a poem or a song

▶ FINDING YOUR PASSION

I refer to passion in this chapter as that powerful feeling for doing something you love. Those experiences that bring you happiness in life and make you feel alive regardless of how good you are at them. These could be anything from singing, exercising, reading, working or spending time with others or traveling. Finding your passion can be a powerful tool to do more of what you love and less of what you don't, perhaps not all the time but at least some of the time. The main thing here is to reflect on what you love and to try to merge it with what you are good at. Knowing and understanding your personal values can help you identify your passion.

Activity

In order to find your passion/s, write on this table the things you love to do on the left column and the things you are good at on the right column. Once you've identified the things you love and the things you are good at, try to see how the two link or could be connected, and write how you think they do in the middle column.

For example, I love writing, and I am good at teaching, so I would put writing about teaching. What you put is up to you, and it may change over time depending on your lived experiences, your capabilities and even where you live in a point in time.

TABLE 7.6 Finding your passion

Things you love to do List all your interests, hobbies	Your passion	Things you are good at List all your skills and strengths

▶ FINDING YOUR PURPOSE

All the activities I have introduced to you in this chapter will point you towards finding your purpose. A major contributor to living a long and fulfilling life is to find your purpose. We each have a different purpose; yours will be unique to you depending on your talents, passion, values and strengths. Purpose is your reason for being – the thing that makes you light up. It is more than a goal, which may be short term, as purpose is something that will fulfil you always. Living a life with purpose is good for your mental and physical wellbeing. It will also help you be connected to others and continuously grow. It may be that your purpose shifts throughout your life based on your circumstances and lived experience. That's absolutely fine and part of your journey. Living your best life and being your best, whatever that may be, are all connected to your purpose. Within this chapter and throughout this book, there are many activities that will help you find your purpose and ignite your passion. Things like practicing gratitude, being kind and having a positive mindset are all helpful to discover your purpose.

Activity

Finding your purpose

Complete the table below by following the steps in this activity. It will help you use all the things you've learned and practiced in this chapter to find your purpose at this time.

TABLE 7.7 Finding your purpose

Steps	Your purpose
1. Overall dream	
2. Personal statement	
3. Road map (WOOP)	
4. Overcoming obstacles	
5. Personal development plan	

1. Think of what you want out of life – your overall dream – and write this down on the top of a page
2. Create your own personal statement by writing a paragraph describing your core values, your top character strengths and your short-term goals and how you see them getting you to your long-term dream. When you are happy with your personal statement, write it down under your dream.
3. Do a road map: think about what you have to do to get there. Be practical; for example, you could use the WOOP (wish, outcome, obstacles, plan) model I introduced you to in Chapter 4
4. Once you have identified your obstacles, think about how to overcome them; be realistic and objective. You could write these below your personal statement.
5. The last step in this activity is to do a personal development plan of how you are going to get to your dream. What are the things you need to learn, do, change or adapt to get you there and be able to live by your purpose?
6. Go back to the top of the table and under the title "your purpose," write what you think and feel your purpose is. With this activity, you will also know how to act on it to make it happen.

▶ LOVE WHAT YOU DO

Being your authentic self by following your passion and your purpose considering your values and using your strengths will enhance your wellbeing regardless of what you do. So remember, don't settle by what others expect of you. Be your authentic self, and live by what matters to you. That's what true success looks like. This may not be the related to the job you do but to the things you like to pursue.

In fact, Marcus Buckingham (2022), an expert on human strengths, argues that finding your true purpose may not be the best way to find a career or job that you love. Instead, he proposes that people should focus on finding within their job the things they love to do and bring them more energy, and to do more of those things within their job. Buckingham calls these activities, which leave them energised and get them into flow (as I covered earlier in this chapter), "red threads" (Buckingham 2022). He argues that by trying to include more of the things you love in your everyday job, you will be happier and healthier. In fact, spending 20% of our time doing the things we love has a positive impact on our wellbeing. So how can people find those red threads? Well, Buckingham (2019) invites people to spend a week identifying the things they love and the things they loathe about their job.

Activity

I have taken this this activity from Buckingham (2019) to get you reflecting on finding the things you love in the job you do.

Take a piece of paper, and write a line along the middle to make two columns. On the top left, write "love it", and on the top right, write "load it". Spend a week paying notice to what you do, and every time you feel in flow or loving what you do, write the activity on the left-hand side of the paper. Every time you find yourself bored with an activity, procrastinating or deflated whilst doing it, write it on the right-hand side of the paper. After that week, you would have identified the things you love to do and the things you don't.

For the following weeks, try to do every day some of the activities you love. Of course, that doesn't mean that you would stop doing the things you don't like, as this would be unrealistic, but is about trying to craft within your job more of the things you love to do. Over time, try to build the things you love to do to be 20% of your time.

▶ OVERVIEW

Within this chapter, I have explored a variety of ideas, tools, theories and activities to help you on your journey to strengthening your occupational wellbeing. By learning about yourself, about what you like and what you are good at, you can start a path towards the types of things you can do in the future. The type of things that will give you joy and help you make a living at the same time, but most importantly to live a fulfilling life of purpose where you can thrive and flourish and, by doing so, live your best life, even if that means changing careers many times. Whilst you are learning about yourself, be curious, open-minded and, above all, have fun!

These are the main areas we explored:

- A definition of occupational wellbeing to help you understand the term and how it relates to your experience
- An overview of your personal values and why it matters to know them and live by them
- The importance of knowing your character strengths to be your best self
- Finding your element to help you thrive doing something you love
- Being in the zone to perform at your best whilst having fun
- The importance of creativity and how to exercise it
- How to find your purpose and the things you love to do to live your best life

I hope you have found the activities and ideas I presented to you in this chapter interesting and useful on your journey to achieve occupational wellbeing.

▶ REFERENCES

Ashinoff, B. K. and Abu-Akel, A. (2021). Hyperfocus: The forgotten frontier of attention. *Psychological Research*, 85(1), 1–19.

Brenebrown.com. (2022). *Dare to lead list of values*. Available from: https://brenebrown.com/resources/dare-to-lead-list-of-values/ [Accessed 13 July 2022].

Buckingham, M. (2019). *Spend a week in love you're your job*. Available from: www.marcusbuckingham.com/spend-a-week/ [Accessed 10 October 2022].

Buckingham, M. (2022). *Love and work: How to ding what you love, love what you do and do it for the rest of your life*. Boston: Harvard Business Review.

Csikszentmihalyi, M. (2002). *Flow: The classic work on how to achieve happiness*. London: Random house.

Gerver, R. (2016). *Simple thinking: How to remove complexity from life and work*. Chichester, West Sussex, UK: Capstone, a Wiley brand.

Peterson, C. and Seligman, M. E. P. (2004). *Character strengths and virtues: A handbook and classification*. Oxford: Oxford University Press.

Petrone, P. (2018). *Why creativity is the most important skill in the world*. Available from: www.linkedin.com/business/learning/blog/top-skills-and-courses/why-creativity-is-the-most-important-skill-in-the-world [Accessed 12 January 2020].

Quinlan, D. M. and Hone, L. (2021). *The educators' guide to whole-school wellbeing: A practical guide to getting started, best-practice process and effective implementation*. Abingdon: Routledge.

Robinson, K. (2001). Mind the gap: The creative conundrum. *Critical Quarterly*, 43(1), 41–45.

Robinson, K. and Aronica, L. (2009). *The element: How finding your passion changes everything*. New York: Viking.

Robinson, K. and Robinson, K. (2022). *Imagine if: Creating a future for us all*. London: Penguin.

VIA Institute of Character. (2020). *The VIA classification of character strengths and virtues*. Available from: www.viacharacter.org/ [Accessed 3 February 2021].

World Economic Forum. (2020). *The 10 skills you need to thrive in the fourth industrial revolution*. Available from: www.weforum.org/agenda/2016/01/the-10-skills-you-need-to-thrive-in-the-fourth-industrial-revolution/ [Accessed 22 January 2021].

Financial wellbeing

Managing your money

▶ INTRODUCTION

In this chapter, I will explore financial wellbeing as a key aspect in getting ready for university. Planning how you are going to be able to afford things and thinking about the steps you have to take to achieve this will help you enjoy your time at university and avoid stress and anxiety. I will explain what financial wellbeing is and why it is important. In this chapter, I will cover:

- A definition of financial wellbeing
- An overview of how financial behaviour can affect your mental health
- An exploration of the social aspects of spending
- A review of the negative habits that can affect your spending
- An in-depth look at budgeting and how to do it
- A real-life case study exploring scams and how to protect yourself from them
- An explanation of how bank accounts, saving accounts and credit cards work
- A definition of a variety of terms related to finances you may encounter

DOI: 10.4324/9781003317548-8

▶ WHAT IS FINANCIAL WELLBEING?

Financial wellbeing is the feeling of having control of your money and feeling secure in the knowledge that you can buy the essential things you need, pay your bills and deal with unexpected situations by being able to afford them.

Research shows that people who experience financial wellbeing are less stressed, and this can have a positive impact on their wellbeing. Financial wellbeing is affected by income, habits, choices, your social environment, family and friends so it is important to check regularly to see what type of expenses may be affecting your income.

Activity

In the following table, reflect on the type of things that can have an impact on your income.

TABLE 8.1 Things that can have an impact on your income

Impact on your income	What type?	How does it affect your income?
Needs		
Habits		
Choices		
Social environment		
Others		

▶ MENTAL HEALTH AND FINANCIAL BEHAVIOUR

According to Fenton-O'Creevy (2022), a researcher looking at the role of emotions in financial decision making found that people who are impulsive buyers may be doing so to avoid thinking about how they feel and are therefore more likely to get into financial problems.

Worrying about money can lead to severe stress, anxiety and seriously affect your mental health. This can become a ruminating problem where you worry about money and then worry about worrying about money. Not being able to manage money properly can make you feel embarrassed or even guilty, especially if you are financially dependent on other people. The key thing is not to avoid thinking about money but to think about money in a proactive way.

As a student entering university, it may be that this is the first time you will need to be responsible for your income and spending. This may not be the case, as you may have already had a job and be quite able to understand and manage your finances. Nevertheless, it is always good to know and understand how to manage money effectively.

The most important things when it comes to financial wellbeing are to be honest with yourself and to avoid worrying about money by keeping on top of your finances and not avoiding thinking about them. Avoiding may be easier to do if you are feeling worried, stressed or low because you will feel relieved for a period of time. The problem is that avoiding thinking about your money will not change your situation, and over time, this will create more anxiety. On top of that, if you don't have control over your expenses, you may get into debt (when you owe money) or arrears (when you are late to pay something) on your bills. These can have serious consequences on your finances and your future ability to borrow money from a bank or to get a credit card, for example.

I am not suggesting that you should only spend money on the basic things and that you should feel guilty or worried when you buy yourself a treat. It is all about balance.

The best way to manage your money is by becoming financially literate. This means to know how to manage your money and to understand what the different types of financial terms mean. It includes things like:

- Understanding money transactions
- Budgeting effectively
- Understanding payslips
- Learning how to pay your bills in time
- Understanding savings and how to save
- Borrowing money responsibly

We will cover some of these in this chapter.

▶ THE SOCIAL ASPECTS OF SPENDING

Spending money is a necessity to some extent as there are basic needs that we need to meet in order to be healthy and well. These are essential and must always take priority. There is also a social aspect to spending. By this, I mean that sometimes, due to peer pressure, you may feel you need to spend money on going out, meals and clothing to keep up with your friends, and if you don't, you may feel left out or as if you are missing out. You may wonder why your classmate or your flatmate can afford all sort of things and goes out all the time and you can't. Or it could also be the other way around; you may be able to live comfortably compared to the people around you. We all come from different backgrounds, with different experiences and different circumstances. Some people you meet may be funded by their parents or have more money, and others will have less, and this should always be respected.

It could also be that what you see on social media may make you feel as if you don't have enough or the best car, clothes, mobile, etc. This can be dangerous as it can lead you into debt, and it can also make you lose a sense of what really matters. If you or someone you know is struggling with money, it is important to seek support. Some universities have some type of financial support, and sometimes students don't know about it, so it is worth checking. As we saw in the socio-emotional wellbeing chapter, we are social beings wired to connect, and part of this connection is about socialising. We have an innate need to be accepted, to belong and to exist within a group. And although there are many activities you could do that would require no money, socialising can be expensive. Therefore, it is important that you are honest with yourself about how much you can spend and stick to it. I will explore budgeting later in this chapter.

Activity

Think about the many fun activities you can do without money, and see if you can share them with a friend. Some examples could be going for a walk in the park or playing board games if you have any.

▶ NEGATIVE HABITS THAT CAN AFFECT YOUR SPENDING

There are certain specific things that you may not be aware that you do but that can affect your spending in a negative way. Here are some of those:

- Spending more than you earn/receive
- Not budgeting
- Overusing your overdraft
- Spending your student loan on non-essential things
- Ignoring subscriptions you no longer need
- Not shopping around but buying something in the first place you see it (especially online)
- Habitual impulse buying (if this is a habit, it may be a symptom of something more that should be explored)
- Paying your bills late
- Not paying your bills
- Not building an emergency buffer (small savings in case of eventualities)

- Delaying payments
- Not checking regularly (daily) your bank account (you can do this online)

So clearly, to manage your finances well, you need to have a budget. I will now explore how to do a budget and stick to it.

▶ BUDGETING

A budget is a financial plan that you make based on your income and expenditure over a period of time. It could be weekly, monthly or however long you want to do it. To create a budget, you need to make sure you have all the information regarding all your income and all your expenses. By creating a budget, you can identify how much money you have going in and out of your bank account and what you need to prioritise to have your basic needs met.

Income

Income is the money you have coming in. To do your budget, first you need to identify every type of income you have coming, for example:

- Student loan
- Any grants, scholarships or bursaries
- Part-time or full-time job
- Benefits (in the UK)
- Family support
- Savings
- Other

Not everyone will have the same type of income. Some people need to work during university whilst others don't, and some will get support from their family whilst other won't.

Also, make sure you don't include as your income any debt like a credit limit on your credit card or your bank overdraft. Make sure that you are clear about how much money you have coming in and when. Some money will come at different times. For example, in the UK, a student loan is paid to students three times per year. A job may pay you weekly, monthly or fortnightly.

Ascertaining how much you will have for the year will depend on when you get the money. So, for example:

Weekly to monthly income can be calculated like this:

Weekly sum × (multiplied) by 52 weeks (one year)/divided by 12 (months in a year)

Example:

£150 × 52 = £7,800/12 = £650

Activity

In the table below, identify the income you have and its amount, and add it all up. Make sure you are consistent on when you get it (weekly, monthly or every three months, for example). Make sure this is income you can rely on a regular basis, so at this point, don't add any presents you may get from friends and family unless this is a regular amount to help you with your expenses.

TABLE 8.2 Calculating your income

Type of income	Amount
For example, part-time job	£300 per month
Total income	

Student loans in the UK

If you are an undergraduate student from the UK starting university, you are entitled to apply for a student loan to help you pay for your tuition fees (paid directly to the university) and a maintenance loan (paid to your bank three times per year) to help you with some of your living costs. The student loan is divided into your tuition fee loan, and how much you get depends on your circumstances, including where you will live as well as your parents' income, if you have parents. This is called means tested, and this is the case unless you are over 25 or estranged from your parents. The less your parents earn, the more you are likely to get. At the time of writing this book, in the UK, you don't need to pay back your student loan whilst you are still a student but rather once you finish your degree and are earning a certain amount of money.

If you have a disability, you can also apply for Disabled Students' Allowance. This is not means tested and considers your individual needs. If you get DSA, you won't get money but the things you need to be able to study. For example, you may get an ergonomic chair, taxis to get to campus or a support worker. If you are a parent or someone with caring responsibilities, there may be other sources of support you can seek.

If you are a postgraduate student, the loans are not means tested. Loans are normally paid in the UK in three instalments based on your chosen university dates. There is extra funding for disabled students in the form of a disability students' allowance grant which doesn't have to be paid back. To be eligible, students will have to go through an assessment to identify the special requirements, and this will depend on their individual circumstances.

To fully understand student loans in the UK, the best place to go to is GOV.UK as they have all the relevant information and links of how and when to apply. You can also find out information there if you are an international student thinking of studying in the UK.

Financial support at university

Universities have a variety of support that may be available to students depending on their circumstances. It is useful to find out about your chosen institution's support and seek it early. Some may be awarded automatically, whilst others will need an application. Here are some examples of the support they may be provided by universities:

* Bursaries: one-off payment to support students in low income or certain personal circumstances
* Hardship loans: one-off payment to students in crisis
* Laptop loans: a scheme that lends you a laptop for the duration of your course
* Scholarships: normally based on achievements such as academic or sport excellence

Outgoings

Once you have identified the amount per week, month or year that you have coming in, you should then look at your outgoings. These are the type of regular payments you must make to meet your basic needs. If you remember, in Chapter 1, I introduced you to Maslow's hierarchy of needs. In it, we identified the deficit needs; those needs that must be met for you to be able to survive. In the following table, you will see the type of basic needs that you will need to consider when you are getting ready to go to university. The ones at the top of the list are those things you cannot avoid as they will help you stay healthy. I have also given you examples of the type of outgoings you will need to take into account. This will be subjective and will depend on your preferences.

A good way to identify essential outgoings is to ask yourself this:

1. Do I need it?
2. Will I use it?

TABLE 8.3 Types of outgoings

Is it a need or a wish?	Outgoings	Consequences of avoiding paying for this
Food	Weekly shopping	Become malnourished
Medicines	Prescription	Become unwell
Self-care • Hygiene products • Self-care products • Haircut • Clothing	Shopping	Could affect your wellbeing, but it is worth questioning if it is a necessity or a luxury
Tuition	Fees	Unable to continue university
Accommodation	Rent	Risk of eviction
Utilities • Water • Electricity • Gas • Internet (broadband/ Wi-Fi) • TV license (in the UK)	Bills	Get into debt or lose access to these
Mobile Phone	Bill	Get into debt Not being able to communicate with others or access important information
Loans	Bills	Get into debt
Socialising	Outings	Isolation
Transport	Bus pass/train tickets/petrol, etc Car insurance	Unable to get to places
Books and supplies	Buy books that are needed	
Other • Magazine • Hobbies • Subscriptions (Netflix, Spotify, Amazon Prime, gym, etc)	Bills	Miss out on entertainment

TABLE 8.4 Calculating your outgoings

Type of outgoing	Amount
Total	

Activity

Create a table like the one above and include all your essential outgoings, making sure the essential items are at the top.

Can you afford it?

Once you have identified your income and outgoings, you need to calculate your disposable income. That is the money you have left over after you have paid all your bills and living outgoings.

Activity

Use the table below to work out how much you have left over by inputting your total income and subtracting your outgoings:

TABLE 8.5 Calculating out your budget

Total income	
Total outgoings	−
Money left over	=

If the amount of money going out exceeds what is coming in, you are in deficit and may get into debt unless you reduce some of your outgoings. If this is the case, don't panic, but think about what you can realistically do to stay within your budget. If there is money after you have done this calculation, that is your disposable money, which is the money you can use to save or to spend on things that may not be a priority.

Spending online

Online shopping has become extremely popular and, even more than ever, allows you to buy anything you need or want from companies all over the world. Shopping online can be good as it allows you to compare items both within sites and between sites. It can be a powerful way to keep your finances in order, and there are lots of very useful sites to help you understand and manage money. I particularly like, and use on a regular basis, Money Saving Expert. This is a site created by Martin Lewis (2022), an expert on all things money and spending. He even has a section for student spending, which I recommend you check as it is very useful to find the best deals and discounts and learn about money and finances. Lewis has done an incredible job and has helped millions of people manage their money better. He also advocates for money literacy, which should be taught in schools. I happen to agree completely with this; from a personal point of view, if I had learned how to manage money when I was younger, it would have helped me a lot, especially once I moved away from home.

There is also a darker side to spending online. It is an activity that can be done 24 hours a day, which may lead to spending more than we have. It can also affect our mental health and can be dangerous for people with addictive personalities or those who gamble. The temptation is always there and very easy to access too, so we need to learn how to manage this so we use it in a healthy way.

Where to do your budget?

It is up to you where you feel more comfortable doing your budget. You could use a notebook, Microsoft Excel, Microsoft Word, a spreadsheet, or even an app. The important thing is to get used to doing it and to stick to it so you don't get into debt that could have been prevented.

Money worries

If you are worried about money, the most important thing is to seek help. Don't suffer alone; this will only make things worse. We all need help sometimes, and there are places that can help you with money worries. Here are some in the UK:

- Citizens Advice Bureau can give advice on debt and benefits: www.citizensadvice.org.uk
- Mental Health & Money Advice is a UK-wide service providing information and advice to individuals with mental health and money worries: www.mhma.org.uk/toolkit
- Turn2Us is a charity providing practical support for people struggling with their money: www.turn2us.org.uk
- Money Saving Expert, as I mentioned before, is a great online resource to learn about money, spending, saving and debt: www.moneysavingexpert.com

▶ BEWARE OF SCAMS

Scams are deceitful schemes that get people to share their information to be used illegally or to steal their money.

Although scams have been around forever, with the rise of online shopping, there has also been a rise in scams. This has become even more prominent during the Covid-19 pandemic with scammers taking advantage of people's worries about Covid.

Scams work in many ways, and they have become very elaborate. For example, scammers can target us through emails, texts, phone calls or online transactions, pretending to be our bank. The problem is that these online scams look extremely realistic, so it is sometimes very difficult to identify which site is real and which is not.

The following list contains some common scams you may come across.

- An email from a lawyer explaining that you have been chosen to receive a large amount of money but need to share your details
- An email from a rich person who you don't know offering to go into business with you

- A direct message from someone pretending to be another person (catfishing)
- A direct message from what appears to be your bank asking you to change your pin
- A direct message from what appears to be the government asking you to pay for a Covid test, as you have supposedly been identified as "at risk"
- A direct message from what appears to be the NHS (National Health Service in the UK) asking you to book your Covid vaccine
- An email from what appears to be your bank telling you about a suspicious transaction
- Adverts on social media promising amazing things for little money
- Text messages which appear to be from the post office asking you to click on a link to pay a fee to get a delivery
- Fake social media emails asking you to verify your accounts
- Pages which have grammatical or spelling errors may not be a scam but should make you question their legitimacy

So what can you do to protect yourself from scams?

- Before answering any messages, requests or emails, make sure they are legitimate. You can do so by clicking on the email sender as this will show you the real email it has come from, for example.
- Make sure you keep your passwords safe and that these comply with the security of the site
- Hover over hyperlinks to see if they are legitimate. A hyperlink that isn't legitimate will look very different as you hover over it, so, for example, the page www.bbc.co.uk might look like www.bbc.xsnvercsn.co.nz.
- Only open an attachment if you know the sender
- Be aware of emails that don't address you by your name
- Ensure payments you make online are secure by checking the webpage credentials.

How do I know if I've been scammed?

Being scammed is a very unpleasant experience; it is scary and can make you feel ashamed. These are some signs that you may have been a victim of a scam:

- You paid for a purchase or service and it never arrives, or the seller goes quiet
- You have unexplained transactions in your bank account or on your credit card
- Your bank calls you to verify if you have done a purchase which seems suspicious
- Your credit score changes dramatically

Case study

CONTENT WARNING

This case study includes an upsetting account that includes references to transphobia. If you are affected by this, please seek help (Mermaids.org.uk 2022).

I've been scammed! This is Sam's story in their own words. Although the story is real, I have changed their name to maintain confidentiality.

It's early February 2022, and I get a text from someone I had been dancing with the night before, saying they had tested positive for COVID. Naturally, I think to myself that I should book a PCR test and, just as I'm thinking that, I get a text from what appears to be the NHS, sending me a link to book a PCR test. It looked just like all the other COVID-related texts I'd received from the NHS, and when I clicked on the link attached, the Website raised no flags either.

For all intents and purposes, I had been contacted by the NHS . . . right? Then things started to get a little fishy. The website told me that I had to pay £1.50 to have the test sent to me. Now, you might be thinking that this would clearly never be the case, and you would have realised at this point that you were being scammed.

Having just been told by a person I knew that I might have COVID though, and receiving this text within the same hour, my first thought was to trust. This couldn't have been a coincidence. As soon as I entered my card details though, I felt off. I called my parents, explaining the situation and asking what I should do, and was told to call my bank and cancel my card immediately, so that's what I did. I could breathe! They hadn't taken any money from my account, and now they couldn't.

As I sat on my bed, thinking about how easily I fell victim to that situation, and how badly that could've gone, I got a call; an 0800 number. It was my bank, calling to tell me that someone had tried to take some money out of my account in another country, but that the transaction had been blocked. That makes sense, I thought, given what had just occurred. They told me that they needed to secure my account even further, and that in order to do so, we needed to move my money into a level 3 security account.

Terrified of it happening again, I did just that. As soon as I transferred the money out of my account though, that same feeling – that something was off – came back, and it came back with a vengeance. I sensed that I had just made a grave mistake. I mean why would they need me to move my money out of my account in order to secure it? So, I googled the number, which you would think I should've done from the start, but it would have made absolutely no difference. It was the bank's actual phone number. Reassured, I stayed on the phone. Now at this point, they said they had to put me on hold in order to secure it.

Five minutes went by, and I asked them if they were still there. Yes, they said, "we're still working on it, just hold on for a little while longer." Then another 5 minutes went by, and the same exchange was had between us. Now 20 minutes into being on hold, I got that feeling for the third and final time. No way would they have me on hold for this long without reassuring me, without explaining to me what was going on at the very least. So, I texted my dad and updated him, hoping for some advice. "Hang up now," was all his response said. Hang up? How could I hang up? I was £800 down (more than my entire budget for the term), and if I hung up then, it would be like admitting defeat. It would be an acceptance that I wouldn't be seeing that money again, something I just couldn't do. Eventually though, I gave in; I finally admitted to myself that this was still the scammers, and when I did, I was overcome with emotion. I called my parents sobbing, screaming down the phone; distraught that I now had no money, and ashamed of how I could have been so naïve. What now?

Now I don't know what those on the other of the phone were doing for those 20 minutes I was on hold, but I suspect it relates to this next part of the story. For whatever the reason I ended the call with my parents, and lay in my bed crying. Little did I know that as I was doing this, my parents were on the phone with "me". After ringing *my* phone number, a man picked up, mumbling answers to my dad's questions so quietly so as not to reveal that it wasn't me. Of course my dad noticed that it wasn't me pretty quickly and, naturally, got very angry with the people on the other end of the line. Knowing their cover was blown, the tone of this crime changed very quickly.

You see, whilst on the phone with me, they kept on calling me "sir," and as a non-binary person, I corrected them as I would do in any similar situation. When the jig was up in the conversation with my dad then, not knowing that my parents already knew I was non-binary, the man started saying things like "are you proud to have a non-binary child?," outing me and putting me into a situation that, with parents less accepting than mine, could have been extremely dangerous. Not only that, but I received texts from them that I only found days later, spouting capitalised transphobia and gross obscenities that cut as deeply as the shame they caused from their scam. Not only did they steal my money, but that day they stole my phone number, my identity, and my sense of security.

Fortunately, I eventually got my money back, and I was privileged enough to be able to borrow enough money from my parents to get me by for the rest of the semester. Both me and my dad had to change our phone numbers though and, moreover, I was – and quite frankly still am – vulnerable, even almost a year later. I can honestly say that I don't feel safe; that at any moment, this could just as easily happen again. Why?

Because before I found myself in this situation, I swore that I was smart enough to never fall for this kind of scams. That I would pick up on all the signs.

They were just *that* good though. And not only that, but the stars aligned for those scammers that day, their victim happening to have a genuine COVID scare within the same hour that they sent out their bait. If it wasn't for that coincidence, perhaps I would not have been so easily fooled, but I can't say for sure. All I know is that you never think it's going to happen to you until it does. I share my story not to scare you, or to make you lose trust and/or hope in everything. I remain an optimist, and someone who believes the best in people. Whilst I don't necessarily feel entirely safe yet, this situation has taught me a lot about vigilance, and the importance of knowing how smart scammers can be. When it comes to money, people will go to, honestly, quite impressive, yet nefarious, depths to acquire it. Being smart is one thing, but when your weaknesses (I.e., fear of getting COVID) are being exploited, it becomes easier than we might like to admit for us to lose our wits. More important than intelligence in these situations, I have learnt, is *vigilance.*

Whenever it comes to your finances, it is okay to take extra time to think through the situation. When I was on the phone, I was made to feel rushed – as if taking my time to think would increase the risk. If you are being rushed to do anything when it comes to your money, think twice about doing that thing, because I can guarantee you that any organisation that genuinely cares about protecting your finances would ensure that you had all the knowledge and resources you need to make an informed decision. I hope that my experience has not been in vain, and that it can be a useful point of reference for what can happen to anyone, no matter who you are. I was awarded a First-Class Honours for my bachelor's degree, and a Distinction in my master's. I am an introspective and socio-emotionally intelligent person. I was also scammed.

Clearly Sam was deeply affected by this experience, and although they eventually got their money back, it has taken time for Sam to feel safe again. These scams can affect people in many ways, and this is why being vigilant is important.

What can I do if I've been scammed?

- Call your bank immediately, make them aware of the scam, and cancel any payments
- Report the scam to the police
- Block any numbers that seem suspicious
- Stop any further communication with the scammers
- Seek support from family, friends or from your university wellbeing support

Activity

For this activity, I want you to think that you are Sam's friend as you answer these questions.

1. What would you say to Sam to help them protect themselves from scammers?
2. What would you do to support Sam following their experience?
3. What will you do to protect yourself from scams following Sam's experience?

▶ BANK ACCOUNTS

As a university student in the UK, you will need to have a current bank account in order for your student loan to arrive. Bank accounts are very different between banks. Some have perks for students such as a rail card if you join their bank or discounts, so it is worth shopping around for the best one for you. You can do this search through Google or go to websites such as Money Saving Expert, Money Supermarket and others that can compare the accounts for you. Some student bank accounts will offer you a free fee overdraft.

Beware of overdrafts

When you open a student account in the UK, you will normally be offered an overdraft as a buffer. This is when your bank lets you spend more money than you have, normally at no extra cost for a set period. They will give you a set amount, and you can choose to take it all, take part of it or not accept it. Whilst this may seem appealing and useful, especially for emergencies, and it is a good idea to have a buffer (a small amount of overdraft as a cushion in case you need it), try not to use it. It is a loan that you will have to pay back later. Many students get into debt by spending their whole overdraft in their first term of university, and this then causes them to be short on money by the end of the year.

Credit cards

Using credit, which is when you have money available to you that has been lent, normally by a bank or building society, can be useful. It can help you buy things you may need, such as a laptop, and pay it in instalments (for example, monthly rather than all at once). However, it is only useful and recommended when you know you will have the money to pay back what you have used and when you feel comfortable with the interest (what the bank charges you for using the credit) you will have to pay on that money.

There are credit cards that offer 0% introductory rates. This means that within a set period, you will not pay interest on what you buy. Once the period has finished, you will be charged interest. So if you have a card with introductory rates, make sure you pay the money back within this period.

As previously stated in this chapter, when you are going to use your credit card, make sure you ask yourself if what you are buying is something you need and you can afford.

Beware of credit card debt

It is easy to lose sight of our spending and to feel that we have a lot of money if our credit card comes with a lot of credit. Credit card bills normally come with a minimum payment requirement.

This is the minimum amount you must pay monthly. If you don't, you may be charged daily interest, which can grow fast, so never avoid paying this amount. If you are having money troubles and can't pay, instead of ignoring it, contact your bank as they may be able to help you.

Saving accounts

These types of accounts allow you to save money and give you interest on your money. That means you will earn some (very small amounts) money for keeping it in the saving accounts. The amount you will get depends on which account you choose as well as the interest rates available at the time. It is always worth checking comparison sites to find the best account for you. This is a useful type of account to, for example, keep your student loan so you don't spend it all at once and so you can keep track of your budgeting. There are many types of saving accounts. Some allow you to take the money out instantly, whilst others lock the money, which means you cannot access it for a certain period. If you are considering opening a savings account, shop around for the best deals. These will be the ones that offer you the most interest for your money.

▶ GLOSSARY OF TERMS

To understand your finances, there are certain terms you may come across, which are important to understand. I wanted to end this chapter with some of the financial terms that you may come across.

- Asset: something which has economic value
- Budget: a financial plan for a period of time that includes your income and expenses
- Gross income: the money you receive from an employer/job before any deductions, including tax or other deductions and contributions
- Income tax: a tax on the money you earn

- Net income: the money you have left over after any deductions from gross income
- Banks: companies that deal with money (lending, borrowing, savings, etc)
- Debt: money you owe someone
- Direct debit: an automated payment method based on an arrangement between you and a company where money is transferred from your account into theirs on a specific date to pay a bill. The amount can change depending on the bill.
- Fixed rate: a type of interest charged on a loan or a mortgage which doesn't change over time
- Interest rate: a percentage on the amount of money you have borrowed from a bank or paid to you for money you have saved on a savings account. It is usually a percentage (%).
- Loan: money you borrow
- Mortgage: a loan you may apply for to buy a property
- Overdraft: a type of credit that may be available to you through your bank account to cover transactions if your balance drops below zero
- Profits: any excess money from sales after covering expenditure
- Secured debt: a type of debt that is linked to an asset, which means that if the borrower doesn't pay the debt back, the asset can be lost
- Unsecured debt: a type of debt that is not linked to an asset
- Company shares: the financial assets that people have as part of owning a company
- Credit ratings: an assessment of how someone manage their money to see how likely they are to get credit
- Inflation: a rise in price levels
- Interest: the percentage rate of a loan, a credit card or a savings account
- Per annum (PA): per year
- Pension: a type of savings to use once you retire from a job
- Private sector: the part of the economy that is not being controlled by the state
- Public sector: the part of the economy that the state controls
- Standing order: a regular payment of the same amount that you pay on a specific date from your bank account

▶ OVERVIEW

In this chapter, I have explored financial wellbeing with a view of supporting you in getting ready for university. I know that for some of you, the topics I have covered will be familiar, especially if you already work or if you are financially literate. For some, however, thinking about budgeting and managing money may be a new challenge. Regardless of your financial wellbeing state, I hope you found this chapter and some of its activities useful. Here are the main things I covered in this chapter:

- A definition of financial wellbeing
- An overview of how financial behaviour can affect your mental health
- An exploration of the social aspects of spending
- A review of the negative habits that can affect your spending
- An in-depth look at budgeting and how to do it
- A real-life case study to explore scams and how to protect yourself from them
- An explanation of how bank accounts, saving accounts and credit cards work
- A definition of a variety of terms related to finances you may encounter

▶ REFERENCES

Lewis, M. (2022). *Income and budgeting*. Available from: www.moneysavingexpert.com/family/ [Accessed 19 July 2022].

Mermaids.org.uk. (2022). *Help and support*. Available from: https://mermaidsuk.org.uk/contact-us/ [Accessed 19 July 2022].

O' Creevy, M. F. (2022). *Emotional finance*. Available from https://emotionalfinance.net/author/mocreevy/ [Accessed 12 June 2022].

9 Conclusion and looking to the future

▶ WELLBEING IS A JOURNEY, NOT A DESTINATION

As I am writing this book, I am recovering from long Covid, the virus that affected all of us in many different ways. The virus that made us pause in fear but gave us the space to reflect on how to build a better world. The remnants of Covid will last many years as we learn to live alongside it and try to get back to a type of normal that, for each of us, will look different. I hope that the lessons we have learned have also shown us collateral beauty and helped us take care of ourselves, others and our environment with kindness, compassion and consciousness of how our actions and behaviours have a real impact.

In this book, I set out to explore the six dimensions of wellbeing and share with you what I have learned through my research and lived experience. I took into account current literature, ideas and theories that can be applied to our own lives and can have a positive impact. Much like anything else we learn, wellbeing is something we have to practice every day to maintain it. Now that you have the tools and knowledge of the things that can positively

DOI: 10.4324/9781003317548-9

impact your wellbeing, I hope you create your own toolkit of the different activities that work for you and that you put them into practice today, tomorrow and every day.

▶ FINAL THOUGHTS

Writing this book was a dream come true for me. I am passionate about the power that knowledge has to change our lives for the better. What you do with this knowledge is up to you. Much like having a bicycle and never using it, or a gym membership and never going to it, having this knowledge but not using it will certainly not do anything, so try the activities, enjoy the suggestions, be curious about what works for you and, most importantly, learn about yourself and how to love yourself. This is something nobody else can do for you. As I mentioned many times within this book, consistency, discipline and a proactive approach will be key to your journey to wellbeing.

Because life is constantly changing and you are continually learning, growing and developing, the things you may need to feel well may change over time, and that's fine. One thing I would say is don't try to tackle every dimension at the same time. This can be overwhelming and demotivate you as you try to do too much. My advice is to use this book as a go-to, when you feel you need to work on an area of your wellbeing, and to integrate the activities as you need them, but once you have integrated them, be consistent to see results. With wellbeing, there are no magic wands, and you will need to, at least at the beginning of your journey, be motivated to practice the activities daily.

▶ POCKETS OF WISDOM

As I conclude this book, I want to leave you with my "pockets of wisdom", those main thoughts that have permeated each chapter regardless of the dimension and that will have a positive impact

TABLE 9.1 Pockets of wisdom

1. You are inimitable, there is nobody else in the world like you and that's amazing, so own it!

2. You are the most important person to you, so learn to love yourself and practice self-compassion

3. Focus on the things you can control, and remember, if you can do something about it, do it; if you can't, let it go

4. Keep a positive mindset by knowing that even when things are hard, better times will come

5. You are the owner of your narrative; how it goes is up to you, so make it a good one

6. Perfection is overrated, unrealistic and unachievable, so try your best; that's good enough

7. Stay true to your values, beliefs and ideals; this will help you sleep at night and feel good about yourself

8. Take care of your basic needs; they are important to your wellbeing

9. What other people think of you is their problem; you work on thinking positive things about yourself

10. Failure, mistakes and falls are part of life; the important thing is to acknowledge them and learn from them

11. Find the collateral beauty when things are hard; this will help you develop your resilience and perspective

12. Be kind, considerate and respectful of others; basically, treat them as you would like to be treated

13. Be curious and willing to learn new things, meet new people and enjoy each experience as if it is the first time

14. If you need help, ask. Everyone needs help at some point, and that's okay.

15. Boundaries are healthy; they will keep you protected, so don't be afraid to put them into practice

16. All emotions are valid, necessary and important; what matters is how you express them and process them, so take time to understand how you feel and label those emotions

17. Doing nothing is also good for us; our body and mind need it

18. We are all different, and that's okay, so let's celebrate diversity and encourage inclusion

19. Do the things that make you happy without guilt; you deserve it

20. Life is a learning journey; embrace it and be your best self, then you will certainly have a positive impact on others, your environment and yourself

on your wellbeing. See them as a call to action and as a way of taking ownership of being well, loving yourself and making a positive impact.

I hope you have enjoyed and learned from this book, and whatever it is you go on to do, I wish you success and that you flourish and thrive as you travel through the wellbeing journey and live your best life.

Useful resources

Health issues

- www.nhs.uk

Better sleep

- www.sleepstation.org.uk ideas to help you sleep better
- www.nhs.uk/live-well/sleep-and-tiredness/why-lack-of-sleep-is-bad-for-your-health/NHS explaining why lack of sleep is bad for your health.

Eating disorders

- National eating disorders (NEDA) www.nationaleatingdisorders.org/every-body-different

Support following a crime

- NHS direct (dial 111)
- The UK police (dial 101 or, if it is an emergency, 999)
- www.galop.org.uk/support LGBT+ people who have experienced abuse and violence
- www.mermaidsuk.org.uk support for transgender youth
- www.rapecrisis.org.uk rape support
- www.victimsupport.org.uk/support after a crime
- www.womensaid.org.uk/domestic abuse support

Support for alcohol and drug abuse

- www.talktofrank.com
- www.drinkaware.co.uk/
- www.drugwise.org.uk/www.keep-your-head.com/assets/2/drugs_staying-safe1.pdf

Mental health and wellbeing support

- www.mentalhealthliteracy.org.
- www.mind.org.uk

Help in a crisis

- Call 999 in the UK
- Call Samaritans 116 123 for free
- National suicide prevention helpline 0800 689 5652
- SANEline 0300 304 7000

Information about neurodiversity

- www.exceptionalindividuals.com

Equality advice

- www.equalityadvisoryservice.com Equality advisory helpline

Information about anti-bullying

- www.anti-bullyingalliance.org.uk
- www.ditchthelabel.org

Character strengths

- www.viacharacter.org/character-strengths link to learn about your character strengths

Support with your finances

- https://mermaidsuk.org.uk support for transgender youth
- www.citizensadvice.org.uk Citizens Advice Bureau can give advice on debt and benefits
- www.mhma.org.uk/toolkit Mental Health & Money Advice is a UK-wide service providing information and advice to individuals with mental health and money worries
- www.moneysavingexpert.com online resource to learn about money, spending, saving and anything to do with finances
- www.turn2us.org.uk provides practical support for people struggling with their money

Index

Note: Page numbers in *italics* refer to figures; numbers in **bold** refer to tables.

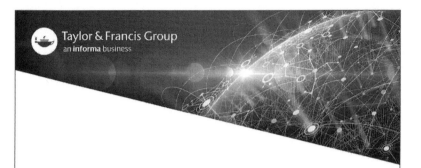